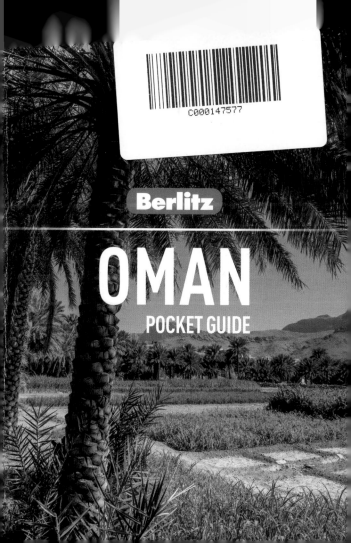

C000147577

# Berlitz

# OMAN
## POCKET GUIDE

## Walking Eye
mobile app

**Discover the world's best destinations with the Insight Guides Walking Eye app, available to download for free in the App Store and Google Play.**

The container app provides easy access to fantastic free content on events and activities taking place in your current location or chosen destination, with the possibility of booking, as well as the regularly-updated Insight Guides travel blog: Inspire Me. In addition, you can purchase curated, premium destination guides through the app, which feature local highlights, hotel, bar, restaurant and shopping listings, an A to Z of practical information and more. Or purchase and download Insight Guides eBooks straight to your device.

INSIGHT ◎ GUIDES

# Walking Eye

◎ DESTINATIONS

⌁ INSPIRE ME

▤ EBOOKS

▦ EVENTS

# **TOP 10** ATTRACTIONS

**SULTAN QABOOS GRAND MOSQUE**
A beautifully designed and decorated contemporary mosque with a capacity for 20,000 worshippers. See page 38.

**NAKHAL FORT**
A soaring structure in the Western Hajar Mountains. See page 50.

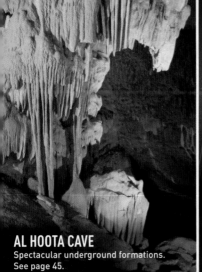

**AL HOOTA CAVE**
Spectacular underground formations. See page 45.

**BAIT AL BARANDA**
This excellent museum traces Muscat's history. See page 33.

**DHOW CRUISE**
Enjoy tranquil bays and stunning views.
See page 79.

**LAND OF FRANKINCENSE MUSEUM**
A fascinating and fragrant history. See page 67.

**RAS AL JINZ TURTLE RESERVE**
Nesting site of endangered green turtles. See page 62.

**SUMHURAM**
The site of an ancient port in a beautiful setting on the banks of Khawr Rawri creek. See page 72.

**MUTRAH CORNICHE AND SOUQ**
The exotic sights, sounds and smells of an authentic Arabian souq. See page 33.

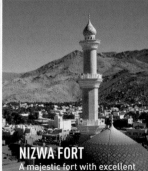

**NIZWA FORT**
A majestic fort with excellent views. See page 42.

# A PERFECT DAY

### 8.00am

## Breakfast

Join the power-walkers and joggers for an early-morning stroll along the quiet beach at Shati al Qurm, followed by a well-deserved outdoor breakfast at D'Arcy's in Jawaharat a'Shati Complex.

### 9.30am

## A mosque visit

Visit the Sultan Qaboos Grand Mosque for a look around this beautifully constructed and exquisitely decorated building, one of the most famous in Arabia. Women must remember to take a scarf to cover their heads.

### 12 noon

## Coastal drive

Drive along the sweeping corniche and through the Muscat Gate into Old Muscat. Admire the facade of the Sultan's Al Alam Palace and take in the latest art exhibition at Bait Muzna Gallery.

### 11.00am

## Local history

Head for Mutrah and spend an hour at Bait al Baranda, a fascinating history museum. Have a hot drink at the Kargeen Caffe before moving on.

### 1.30pm

## Scenic lunch

Drive down the coast to the world-famous Al Bustan Palace Hotel for a superb buffet lunch. The Al Khiran Terrace restaurant offers indoor or outdoor dining with stunning views along the coast, and features 'live cooking stations' for personal freshly cooked dishes.

# IN MUSCAT

**6.30pm**

### A short stroll and an aperitif
Disembark and walk along the Corniche for early-evening drinks on the tiny top-floor terrace of the Marina Hotel. Enjoy fabulous views along Mutrah Corniche to the fort and beyond.

**10.00pm**

### Late-night jazz
Take a taxi back through town to the Park Inn at Al Khuwayr for some late-evening live jazz or lounge music at its laidback Sama Terrazza rooftop bar. Enjoy extensive night-time views towards the Sultan Qaboos Grand Mosque.

**4.00pm**

### Dhow cruise
Return to Mutrah Corniche to board a pre-booked sunset dhow cruise. Glide out of the harbour and along the coast into the bay of Old Muscat, often accompanied by dolphins, and take in views of the Sultan's Palace and the Portuguese forts of Al Mirani and Al Jalali.

**8.00pm**

### Dinner with a view
Reserve a table at La Brasserie, next door to the Marina Hotel, for exquisite French cuisine specialising in fish dishes. This small restaurant is spread over three floors, with the upper terrace having great views across the harbour and fish market.

# CONTENTS

# INTRODUCTION

Oman's potential as a tourist destination is still unfolding, but all the right ingredients are here: unspoilt landscapes, wonderful beaches, a rich culture and friendly people. Oman occupies the southeastern corner of the Arabian peninsula, straddling the Tropic of Cancer along the coast of the Indian Ocean and the Arabian Gulf. It has land borders with the UAE, Saudi Arabia and Yemen, and an area of just over 300,000 sq km (115,800 sq miles), making it slightly larger than Italy. Recent figures show that Oman has a population of some 4,741,305 people; a dramatic increase from the December 2010 census which showed a total population of 2,694,094, with the majority living in Muscat or along the Batinah Coast enjoying year-round sunshine. Foreigners (mostly guest workers) account for 12.5 percent of the population.

## VARIED LANDSCAPES

One of your first impressions of Oman will be the vast stretches of colourful flowers that line the sweeping highways. Armies of imported workers tend the millions of petunias, marigolds, bougainvillea and oleander that offer pleasant urban driving. Beyond the city limits is a good network of coastal roads giving access to the cooler mountainous interior. Ample groundwater flows from these mountains providing 90 percent of requirements, distributed

### Frankincense

There are over 300 types of incense trees, but the best-quality frankincense comes from the tree *Boswellia sacra,* known as silver frankincense. It grows abundantly in the Dhofar region, as does myrrh, of which *Commiphora myrrha* produces the best quality.

through the ancient system of *falaj* water channels, numbering around 40,000 – the longest of which is almost 10km (6 miles).

More than 2,100km (1,300 miles) of coastline stretch from the strategically important Strait of Hormuz, along the Gulf of Oman and Indian Ocean, to the Gulf of Aden in the south. Around the Musandam peninsula in the north and the province of Dhofar in the south, the coast is lined with steep,

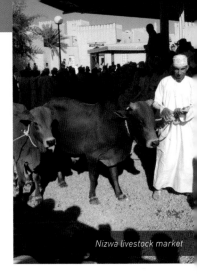

*Nizwa livestock market*

rugged cliffs, interspersed with small sandy bays. Between them is a gentler coastal stretch of shallow bays and sandy beaches, which attract a variety of wildlife, including the endangered green turtle which nests here. In Dhofar, a quirk of nature turns an otherwise searing summer coastline into a cool, misty rain-soaked landscape as the *khareef* monsoon brushes the Arabian peninsula at this one spot between June and September.

The Hajar Mountains stretch from the border with the UAE for some 500km (310 miles) down to Sur, rising to over 3,000m (9,800ft) in the Jabal Akhdar (Green Mountain) massif at the centre of the range. The verdant mountain-tops and deep wooded valleys shelter a rich variety of flora and fauna.

The coastline between Muscat and the UAE border is the flat wide Batinah coast, dotted with impressive castles and large irrigated farms. South of Muscat towards Sur is a more rugged landscape of unbroken grey-sand beach, lapped by a gentle sea

*The exquisite beach at Salalah*

– yet the plain, never more than a kilometre wide, is still extensively cultivated, particularly with date plantations.

Beyond lies the stark, inhospitable landscape of Wahibah and the Empty Quarter deserts. But the desert is also a great preserver, with valuable oil reserves lying below the surface, waiting to be discovered. Petroleum Development Oman (PDO) controls almost all of Oman's oil industry and employs the second-largest number of workers after the government.

## LAND OF TRADITIONS

Modern Oman is embracing responsible tourism and is fast gaining a reputation as a destination for the discerning tourist wanting quality hotels, good food and adventure. The varied terrain and coastline offer unlimited adventures – 4x4 thrills in the gorges and deserts; mountain trekking; scuba-diving in clear seas teeming with fish; dhow sailing and plenty more besides.

Oman's strategy has always been to target the luxury end of the tourist market, and it looks set to continue with plans to build more upmarket resorts. But alongside high-end hotels and adventure travel, Oman also offers a taste of an older, pre-oil Arabia in its souqs and villages.

Everyday life in Oman is still very traditional in many respects. The Omanis succeed in mixing modern life with established social traditions, taking delight in their culture and heritage, and recognising the importance of preserving them. Attending the Friday livestock market at Nizwa is like stepping back in time. Women in burqas watch the bustling crowd of men amidst heated negotiations, much as they have done for hundreds of years. As they depart in modern pickups and 4x4s, the recent change in their lives is obvious.

## ISLAM IN OMAN

Most Omanis follow Ibadism, a particular brand of Islam, distinct from the Shia or Sunni forms, which has played a crucial role in the country's history. As in much of the Islamic world, Islam introduced a new and fervent intellectual debate into people's lives, centring on God's law and the organisation of society. This was especially true of Ibadism in Oman, and it was to produce an extensive Omani literature, particularly rich in law and history.

Islam, meaning 'submission', shapes the principles of government and permeates all aspects of believers' public and private lives,

### Jirz axes

Some of the men wandering around Khasab still carry the traditional small axe known as a *jirz*. Used since ancient times, it is both a useful tool and a walking stick, with the diminutive axehead often embellished with engravings or inlaid brass.

laying down rules for everyday conduct and social relationships. The faithful express their belief without self-consciousness wherever they happen to be.

The people of the coast of Oman and the Emirates have been exposed to a great deal of foreign influence, whether as seafarers along the coasts of India and East Africa, or at home where foreign trading communities have grown up. This has led them to tolerate religious differences, but without abandoning their own traditions and beliefs.

Most tourist itineraries will include a visit to the vast Sultan Qaboos Grand Mosque in Muscat, the only mosque in Oman that non-Muslims are permitted to visit.

## BUILDING A FUTURE

Oil wealth arrived late in Oman compared with Saudi Arabia and the UAE, but it has been put to good use in the past four decades by Sultan Qaboos, who has steered the country through rapid but controlled development. This is now a modern nation, strong and respected by its neighbours. As well as exporting large quantities of its own oil, Oman's unique position puts it in control of more than half the world's oil supply, which passes through the strategically important Strait of Hormuz. Like Dubai and Abu Dhabi, Oman has to perform a delicate balancing act between rapid growth from unsustainable oil revenues, and diversifying into non-oil-based industries, including sustainable tourism.

Under the leadership of Sultan Qaboos, an ambitious programme of education and training is geared to the long-term aim of putting Omani people into many of the jobs currently filled by foreigners. It is hoped this 'Omanisation' will create a sustainable future for the country and further enhance Oman's reputation for quality and innovation, whilst retaining the strong heritage and culture that makes it unique.

# A BRIEF HISTORY

Oman's unique position between Africa and Asia places it at the centre of human development and the spread of early civilisation. Trade contacts with ancient Egypt, Mesopotamia and the Indus Valley highlight the importance of this location, which has been a blessing and a hindrance throughout its history. Persian dominance dictated Oman's subsidiary role for more than 2,000 years, and then came the Portuguese, who dominated international trade in the Gulf and Indian Ocean for over a century. After the expulsion of the Portuguese in the 17th century, Oman controlled its own destiny, even though coastal Muscat and interior Nizwa were often battling for supremacy. Islam, of course, has played a crucial role in the country's history. But the speed and scale of change brought about by the discovery of oil in the Arabian Gulf in the 1950s was unprecedented in world history.

Map of the Arabian peninsula, c.1575

## PREHISTORY

Recent archaeological explorations of Oman have revealed a rich and varied ancient history. Archaeological surveys indicate a constantly changing mosaic of coastal and inland settlements, but many of the earliest sites

*A falaj water channel*

lie along the shores of the Gulf of Oman. The area around Taqah in Dhofar is particularly rich in fossils, especially of early primates from around 30 million years ago, when Arabia was connected to Africa. Dating is difficult, but it could indicate that Arabia was more important in primate development than previously thought. Many sites in southern Arabia had a climate suitable for human settlement. Evidence of early migration from Africa around 125,000 years ago has been found near Mudayy (about 80km/50 miles inland from Mughsayl) in Dhofar.

Until about 16,000 years ago, when sea levels began to rise, the area now occupied by the Gulf would have formed a river valley extending as far as the Strait of Hormuz. The shoreline would have been distant from its present location and 100–150m (330–490ft) lower than the present day average sea level. When the level began to rise it created a variety of coastal landscapes, including the fjord-like coastline of the Musandam peninsula, the plain of the Batinah and the steep cliffs extending from north of Muscat south past Ras al Hadd. These varied marine habitats afforded a glut of easily obtained fish and shellfish. Mangroves attracted birdlife which could be hunted, and adjacent inland areas supported gazelle and, later on, grazing for sheep, goats and cattle. The earliest manmade objects, dating as far back as the 5th millennium BC, have been unearthed at coastal settlements such as Ras al Hamra near Qurm. Excavation of 'shell middens' here has revealed the ground plan of small groups of circular buildings, indicated by stone foundations or arrangements of post-holes. Other finds, such

## ⊘ THE *FALAJ* WATER SYSTEM

The most precious commodity for any settlement in Arabia is water. It is unclear whether the *falaj* system, an ingenious ancient irrigation system, originated in Arabia or Persia. The history of the *falaj* (plural *aflaj*) began around 3,000 years ago, when underground channels were dug by hand to transport water from the mountains to villages and farmland from mother wells dug into the water table. Vertical shafts allow ventilation and the removal of silt and stones carried down the channel. In Oman the best ancient examples are found on the lower slopes around Jabal al Akhdar. Because *aflaj* were so vital in these inhospitable areas they were often protected by watchtowers, as an entire settlement such as Nizwa could quickly be defeated by cutting off its water supply. The job of digging and repairing the *falaj* is highly skilled and traditionally a specialisation of Oman's Awamir tribe, who have the nerve and agility required to work underground in small tunnels full of dust.

A 13th-century illustration of a merchant's dhow

as those at the Neolithic sites of Ras al Jinz and Sur, show that the inhabitants were adept at making stone tools and artefacts.

## EARLY CIVILISATIONS

The Mesopotamian civilisation at Ur in Sumeria (now southern Iraq) lacked metal ores such as copper, which they imported from the Wadi Jizzi region of Oman, inland from Sohar. A clay tablet found at Ur describes an amount equating to 20 tonnes of copper arriving from 'Magan' (northern Oman). Copper smelted around Arja, Beidha and Lusayl could easily be carried down Wadi Jizzi to the port at Sohar before being transported around the Gulf. However, a more direct route ran via Buraymi Oasis and Umm An Nar, the old trading island off the coast of Abu Dhabi. During the so-called Umm An Nar period (2,600–2,000 BC), the copper was taken along the Gulf coast to ancient Dilmun (Bahrain) and thence to the Sumerian cities.

As imported iron replaced copper through the 1st millennium BC, the old copper-working sites of Oman were abandoned. Instead, gold, cornelian, spices, animal hides and oils were carried along the trade routes. Around this time the domestication of the camel improved desert trade and communication. The invention of the *falaj* system also increased food production and led to a rise in population in these well-watered places at the base of the Hajar Mountains.

Meanwhile in Dhofar, the controlled cultivation and distribution of aromatic gum resins, particularly frankincense, can be dated back as far as 1,000 BC. Under the control of the Queen of Sheba, great desert cities like Ubar and the port at Sumhuram sent these precious goods to the temples of ancient Egypt. But the clever Omani merchants had also mastered the seasonal monsoon winds and were trading with Southeast Asia and East Africa, importing spices, silk, ivory, animal skins and slaves.

From the 6th century BC, the dominant power was Persia, with an empire extending to Egypt and India. The Persians controlled Sohar, which for most of its history was far more important than Muscat. By the time of Greek and then Roman dominance, trade from Ethiopia, southwest Arabia and India into the Near East and Mediterranean was in full swing, much of it by camel caravan along the great land routes of the Arabian peninsula. From the 3rd century BC the region fell under Greek influence as they pushed eastwards through Asia. By 250 BC the Parthians (from northeastern Iran) controlled all sea trade and established themselves as the middle men in the development of the silk trade from China, both overland and by sea. During the Sassanid rule of Persia in the 5th century sea trade was back in the hands of Persian seamen, who successfully fought both the Romans and the Arabs for regional control.

## ARRIVAL OF ISLAM

The year AD570 is highly significant in Oman's history. It is the year the prophet Muhammad was born in Mecca (in Saudi Arabia), and the year the great dam at Marib (in Yemen) finally collapsed – Marib was the capital of the Kingdom of Sheba, which controlled the trade of frankincense from Dhofar. The abandonment of Marib by the Azd tribes resulted in the gradual migration – of the Azdi Umani tribe in particular – along the incense trade route into Oman. They settled at the port of Qalhat near Sur and under their leader, Malik Bin Fahim al Azd, ousted the occupying Sassanians and asserted control over eastern trade with India.

Islam spread along the established desert trade routes and is said to have been introduced into Oman during the lifetime of the Prophet Muhammad. The Prophet sent early Islamic emissaries from Medina to all the tribes and settlements of Arabia. The one he sent to Oman was the general Amr Ibn al As. Though Amr targeted the flourishing Persian port and capital of Sohar on the Omani coast, it was the Arab tribal ruling family, the Al Jalenda, and not the Persian governor, who accepted his message. There are several mosques in Oman claiming to exist from the lifetime of the Prophet, including the Al Midhamr mosque at Samail, between Nizwa and Muscat. Even though they have been rebuilt many times, all of these early mosques lie on important pre-Islamic trade routes.

### Jewel of Muscat

A major feat of engineering was the reconstruction of a 9th-century Arab sailing ship using traditional methods at Qantab boatyard near Muscat. Between February and July 2010, an Omani crew successfully sailed the 18m (59ft) *Jewel of Muscat* across the Indian Ocean to Singapore, retracing part of the historic maritime trade route between Arabia and the Far East.

Within the first few decades of Islam, the tribes chose to follow the Ibadi school (distinct from Sunni or Shia), founded by Jabir Ibn Zaid al Azdi from Nizwa. It remains the dominant form of Islam in Oman today. Inter-Islamic conflicts ended with a period of relative peace at the beginning of the 9th century which lasted more than 300 years.

*The Jewel of Muscat*

## MARITIME TRADE

In medieval times, the main port of Sohar prospered greatly under the Abbasid caliphs of Baghdad, as its ships traded around the Indian Ocean and further east to China. Sohar's intrepid sailors are said to have inspired the legend of Sindbad. Around 1330 the Muslim traveller Ibn Battuta described Muscat as 'a small place' when compared to the greatness of Sohar and Qalhat, another prosperous port near Sur. On his way overland to Mecca he stopped at Nizwa, capital of the interior, which he reports as being under the control of tribal kings known as the Bani Nabhan, while the coast was back under Persian rule. Since then, control of the country has been a constant tussle between a coastal hereditary sultan and an interior elected imam.

Portuguese navigators sailed around the Indian Ocean in the early 16th century, making great use of Oman's existing seafaring knowledge. They occupied Muscat and defended it with the forts that can still be seen today. After almost 150 years the Portuguese were eventually expelled by Sultan Ibn Saif al Ya'arubi, who also seized Portuguese territories in East Africa and developed a lucrative slave trade.

## THE OMANI EMPIRE

Following internal conflict, the country was united by Ahmed Ibn Said who started the Al Bu Said dynasty, which has endured to this day. Through a succession of largely popular rulers, Oman increased its sea trade by attacking and occupying overseas territories in the Gulf and East Africa until Zanzibar became the centre of Oman's slave trade. Through the 1830s Sultan Said Bin Sultan extended the empire to its greatest size and made Zanzibar his capital. Agreements were concluded with European powers, and Oman became the first Arab country to establish diplomatic relations with the USA in 1833. But fortunes reversed when the British banned slavery in the same year, after which Oman's economy collapsed.

British support of the Al Bu Said rulers angered many of the nearby Gulf States which were constantly at war with the Al Bu Said over interior territories. British ships came under threat until they concluded a truce with all the local coastal tribes, declaring them the 'Trucial States'. The development of the steamship and opening of the Suez Canal in 1869 left Oman isolated, as larger vessels could bypass its ports and travel directly to India from the Red Sea.

## CREATION OF MODERN OMAN

Internal dissatisfaction by followers of the imam in Nizwa (supported by the Saudis) led to British support of the Al Bu Said rulers in Muscat until the Treaty of Seeb in 1920, which divided

*British troops outside Nizwa Fort, 1957*

control between the 'Imam of the Muslims' and the 'Sultan of Muscat and Oman'. New tribal alliances were formed by Sultan Said Bin Taimur in 1955, when he drove from Dhofar across the desert to Nizwa to assert control, protect Oman's oil interests and force the retreat of the imam. He continued on to Buraymi in order to strike a deal with the Abu Dhabi ruler that split Buraymi/Al Ain, straddling the Oman/UAE border, in half. Further skirmishes caused uncertainty to oil prospecting in the Buraymi region, leading to the 'Jabal Akhdar Incidents' which finally ended resistance to the Sultan's rule, not least with bombing raids by Britain's RAF. Oman changed for ever when oil was finally struck at the Natih Field in 1963.

In the mid-1960s the separatist movement to oust the British from Aden spilled over from South Yemen and became known as the Dhofar Mutiny in Oman. It was eventually put down after a decade with help from Britain's SAS.

Omani at the Sultan
Qaboos Grand Mosque

When he took over from his father in 1970 Sultan Qaboos embarked on a much-needed modernisation programme. When he came to power there were only three schools, two graded roads and one hospital in the whole country, no newspapers, radio or television, and no civil service. Over the last 40 years, Oman has been transformed, through oil and gas earnings, into a land with public electricity and water, even in remote villages, and hospitals, schools and universities around the country. The average life expectancy has risen from 47 to over 70. Diverse tribal groups separated by hundreds of kilometres have now been connected by a network of good roads, creating a greater sense of national unity.

The unrest that swept across the Arab world in early 2011 encouraged demonstrations in Sohar and other parts of the country against unemployment and representation, rather than against Sultan Qaboos himself. Police broke up sit-ins and leaders of the demonstrations were punished, then later pardoned by the Sultan in 2013. Plans to curb the recruitment of foreign workers and increase the minimum wage were also announced.

The rapid progress made over the last decades is there for all to see. Oman is now a modern Arab country, yet one that still retains its own traditions and identity.

# HISTORICAL LANDMARKS

**5,000 BC** Early human settlements along the coast.

**2,500 BC** Copper trade from 'Magan' to Mesopotamia.

**1,000 BC** *Falaj* system of underground water channels developed; frankincense traded from Dhofar to ancient Egypt.

**6th century BC** Persian Empire controls the region.

**3rd–6th century AD** Migration of Azd tribe from Marib into Oman.

**AD 570** Birth of Prophet Muhammad and final destruction of Marib Dam.

**628** Islam arrives in Oman. First mosque built at Samail.

**9th century** Sohar prospers under control of the Abassid caliphate.

**1330** Arab geographer and writer Ibn Battuta travels through Oman.

**1507** Portuguese control the major ports.

**1650** Expulsion of Portuguese by Sultan Ibn Saif al Ya'arubi.

**1744** Ahmed Ibn Said starts the Al Bu Said dynasty.

**1830s** Greatest extent of Omani Empire with its capital at Zanzibar.

**1853** 'Trucial States' peace treaty concluded with the British.

**1955** Sultan Said Bin Taimur reunites 'Oman and Muscat' with Nizwa.

**1963** Oil first discovered at the Natih Field.

**1970** Sultan Qaboos takes control of Oman from his father Sultan Said.

**1981** Oman is founder member of the GCC (Gulf Co-operation Council).

**2001** The Sultan Qaboos Grand Mosque opens in Muscat.

**2011** Demonstrations in Sohar, Sur, Muscat and Salalah following unrest.

**2012** Following a crackdown of the opposition, more than 30 activists are sentenced to imprisonment.

**2013** Sultan Qaboos pardons all activists.

**2014** A ban on recruiting foreign workers takes effect. Sultan Qaboos undergoes medical treatment in Germany.

**2015** Oil production exceeds 1 million barrels per day for the first time.

**2016** Archaeologists working off Al Hallaniyah Island identify a shipwreck, believed to be that of the *Esmeralda* from Vasco da Gama's 1502–3 fleet.

**2017** Oman introduces an eVisa system to help facilitate the expected 25 percent increase in tourists by 2020.

**2018** The Oman Rail network is expected to be completed.

The golden dome of the Sultan Qaboos Grand Mosque

# WHERE TO GO

Almost all visits will start and end in the Omani capital, Muscat, either at the airport or the harbour. Muscat makes a good base for exploring the north: the mountainous interior around Nizwa, the flat Batinah coast, and the rugged east coast to Sur. Dhofar and Musandam are the southern and northern extremities of the country, easily reached by internal flights from Muscat or lengthy road trips. As the roads are continually upgraded, there are more routes and possible circuits for non 4x4 vehicles. Visitors from the UAE can drive directly into Musandam or choose to fly or drive into Muscat.

## MUSCAT

The tranquil Old Town of **Muscat** ❶ clings to a small natural harbour, its hidden inlets legendary for their forts, palaces and souqs. In the neighbouring bay, less than 3km (2 miles) along the coast road, is the port of Mutrah, where bustling markets echo with the calls of traders selling their fish, frankincense and fine silks. Old Muscat is a quiet place to wander, retaining many of its traditional houses and mosques. Although opportunities for tourism abound in Mutrah, the port caters primarily for trade and local fishermen. But the corniche has a few hidden gems leading from it.

Old Muscat and Mutrah are just fragments of modern Muscat. Since the 1970s, the city has grown with the help of oil money, and new business and office districts have sprouted in all directions. Modern highways and flyovers cut through a dramatic topography, leading from one tranquil district to the next up the coast towards Seeb International Airport and into the neighbouring valleys. The main commercial and development has occured in Ruwi, the Central District; Qurm is where the shopping complexes are concentrated; Medinat Qaboos is a mainly residential area; and Al Khuwayr is a district of ministerial buildings and embassies.

## OLD MUSCAT

Although Muscat's foundation dates from the 1st century AD, the town didn't gain recognition until the 14th and 15th centuries, when it attracted traders. In the 16th century it drew the Portuguese, who developed Muscat as their principal naval base and strengthened its defences – until 1650 when they were ousted by an Omani force.

The approach to the old walled city is via the coast road which leads uphill to the Gateway. This reconstructed entranceway

Al Alam Palace

spanning the main road houses the **Muscat Gate Museum** (tel: +968 9932 8754; Sun–Thu 8am–2pm), a room full of information panels on Omani history and traditions.

Old Muscat is home to some fabulous old houses and mosques and is easily viewed on foot. In the heart of its winding streets one of the historic houses has been converted into a fine museum. **Bait al Zubair** Ⓐ (tel: +968 2208 4700; www.baitalzubairmuseum.com; Sat–Thu 9.30am–6pm; no photography) in Al Saidiya Street houses impressive displays and collections. The sections on women's jewellery, adornment and clothing are particularly informative, with superb examples. Differences in regional dress for men are also explained, and the collection of old *khanjars* (Omani daggers), some made entirely of gold, is worth a look. The latest addition is a series of scaled models of famous forts around the country. The comfortable coffee shop is in another restored old house, and the extensive souvenir shop offers a range of books and upmarket gifts, such as frankincense-scented candles, quality replicas of the museum's jewellery and the full range of Amouage perfumes. Space around the Bait al Zubair is used for temporary art exhibitions and displays.

Across the road, the former royal residence of Sultan Qaboos's aunt Muzna has been converted into the sleek **Bait Muzna Gallery** Ⓑ (tel: +968 2460 7006; www.baitmuznagallery.com; Sat–Thu 9.30am–7pm; free), an attractive setting for high-quality Omani-inspired art and design, with the occasional poetry reading or gallery talk (check website for details). In 2016, the gallery began branching out into the art film and digital art world. It currently has its own cinema room, photography studio and residency rooms for visiting artists.

Several fine 18th-century buildings have served as embassies and consulates. Among those still standing is the Bait Fransa, the residence of French consuls until 1920, now the **Omani-French Museum** (Sun–Thurs 8am–1.30pm, Sat 9am–1pm; tel: +968 9334 1903), commemorating Oman's historical links with France. French ships carrying spices and sugar from the Indian Ocean had called at Muscat since the 17th century, and in the 19th century trade links intensified.

The centrepiece of Old Muscat is the **Al Alam Palace ©**. The 1970s architecture of the official Sultan's residence clashes somewhat with the surrounding buildings. The story-book facade can be viewed through the gates at the end of the pedestrianised street. The roof seems to be held up by a series of giant golf tees painted in blue and gold. The other side of the palace looks out over the narrow bay, protected by two hilltop forts, both legacies of Portuguese control in the 16th century. Access to the bay is along a road that passes the blue and white Al Khawr mosque.

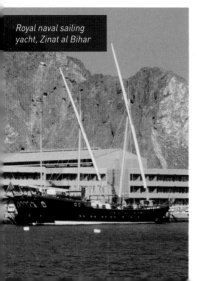

*Royal naval sailing yacht, Zinat al Bihar*

Towering above it is the western fort of **Al Mirani**, completed in 1587. The eastern fort on the other side of the palace, **Al Jalali**, completed in 1588, was formerly the city jail. Neither fort is open to the public.

The white building at the other end of the ceremonial boulevard leading to the royal palace is the **National Museum D** which opened in 2016. With 14 permanent galleries presenting 10,000 years of Omani history and numerous interactive and audio visual displays, it is the Sultanate's premier cultural institution and the first museum in the Middle East accessible for people with visual and physical disabilities. The museum also boasts lecture halls and an 80-seat theatre.

At the far end of the bay are the small dockyards for the magnificent Royal Navy of Oman sail training vessel Shabab Oman and yacht Zinat al Bihar that sail around the world promoting Omani seamanship.

## SOUTH OF OLD MUSCAT

The road south from Old Muscat skirts around the harbours of Sidab and Haramil until it drops down to Marina Bander Ar Rawdah, home of the Marine Fisheries and Science Centre and **Aquarium** (tel: +968 2473 6449).

Continue along the same road to the roundabout with a full-size wooden boat in the centre. This is the *Sohar*, a replica of a 9th-century dhow built for British adventurer Tim Severin's expedition to retrace the sea journey of the legendary Omani sailor Sindbad (see page 59).

Beyond the roundabout, standing majestically in its own bay is the **Al Bustan Palace Hotel** (www.ritzcarlton.com; tel: +968 2479 9666). Luxuriously elegant, it is regularly voted one of the top hotels in the Middle East, and is a real treat for non-resident visitors to look around. Sadly this is not the case for the more

Mutrah fish market

distant Shangri-La Barr al Jissah Resort (www.shangri-la.com/muscat/barraljissahresort; tel: +968 2477 6666), which discourages casual visitors by making it impossible to park anywhere nearby, so best to get dropped off by taxi.

Between the two resorts is the excellent **Oman Dive Centre** (tel: +968 2482 4240), situated in its own idyllic shallow inlet, and the picturesque fishing village of **Qantab**, which still retains much of its local flavour.

## MUTRAH

Mutrah and Old Muscat are connected by a coastal road that twists around jagged mountains and bays. From the frantic early-morning activity of the fish market to the laidback atmosphere of an evening stroll around the souq, the wide expanse of Mutrah harbour is always busy and full of life. Your first stop should be the **fish market**, a lively spectacle. Despite sometimes being outnumbered by tourists, the fish-sellers always seem happy to pose for photos. Early arrival is advisable, as it gets less busy through the day. On the other side of 'Fish' roundabout (the start of the corniche) is the **Bait al Baranda** ❸ (http://baitalbaranda. mm.gov.om/index.htm; tel: 968 2471 4262; Sat–Thu 9am–1pm, 4–6pm), 'the house with the veranda' museum covering the history of Muscat and Oman – from geology, prehistory and early man through to Islam, colonisation and the modern state.

Walking along **Mutrah Corniche**, with the sea on one side and the backdrop of old buildings and mountains on the other, is one of Muscat's great pleasures. Old merchants' houses, gold shops and fruit-juice shops line the roadway around the main

## ⊙ THE C38 TRAIL

This trek quickly transports you from the bustling corniche into remarkably quiet and rugged terrain. Marked by yellow/ white/red-painted signs, the 90-minute trail climbs a total of 150 metres (490ft) before returning to sea level at Mutrah. The walk begins in Riyam Park – pick up the coloured markers in the parking area. From behind the small mosque, follow the stone steps and rusty pipeline to the top of the hill. The views from the high ground are splendid. Beyond the abandoned village the trail then descends a narrow wadi bed with smooth and slippery stones, to Mutrah. Good walking boots, water and a hat are essential. Do not trek alone and take great care on this isolated but worthwhile route. If starting from Mutrah, turn right off the corniche along Way 805 with Bank Muscat on the corner. Go straight over the crossroads signposted 'Wadi Khalfan St' until you see a large concrete dam. Follow a path into a cemetery on the right and ascend from here.

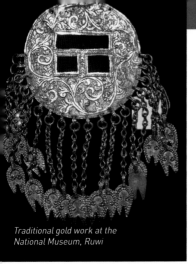

*Traditional gold work at the National Museum, Ruwi*

souq entrance, overlooked by the tiny and wonderfully laidback Al Cornish café. Though modern (concrete booths replaced the original palm structures in the 1970s), the narrow lanes of the **Mutrah Souq** (tel: +968 9827 7478; open daily 8am–1pm and 4–10pm also known as **Al Dhalam** (Darkness) **F**, imbued with the scent of frankincense and sandalwood, bustle with traders, money-changers and shoppers eager to do business. The souq, one of the most authentic in Arabia, has specialist sections for gold, perfumes, silk, leather, jewellery and countless other goods, punctuated by *halwa* (sweetmeat) sellers and coffee shops. Unlike many other Middle Eastern cities, there is little hassle and you will always be treated courteously. Free public toilets are located beside the main souq entrance.

Be sure to observe the 'Residents Only' notices asking tourists not to visit the nearby **Lawatiya quarter**, dominated by the beautiful blue and white decorated Lawati mosque, which houses a Shia sect of the same name. Their residential area is walled and off-limits to outsiders.

The **Mutrah Fort** dominates the end of the first section of Corniche. Nearby is the **Ghalya's Museum of Modern Art G** (tel: +968 2471 1640; www.ghalyasmuseum.com; Sat–Fri 9.30am–6pm). The Old House exhibition portrays what life was like for Omanis between 1950 and 1975, a transformative period of the country's history. A modern art gallery, showcasing Omani and international artists, and a clothes museum presenting traditional local and regional costume are due to open on the same site. You can continue the 3km (2-mile) coast walk to the Gateway into Old Muscat, but it takes about an hour and can get very hot.

**Riyam Park** and **Kalbuh Park** (Sat–Wed 4–11pm, Thu–Fri open all day; free) are popular for a sunset stroll. For the fit and adventurous there is even a short hike that completes a circuit from Riyam Park back to Mutrah through the rough mountain terrain (see page 33).

## RUWI

Separated from the Mutrah Corniche by low mountains is the Mutrah (or Central) Business District (MBD or CBD), developed in the 1970s and home to most of the banks, airlines and travel agencies. Apart from one or two museums worth visiting, the main reason to come to this area is the wide range of restaurants, mainly aimed at office workers.

To the north of the district, the small Bait al Falaj Fort, built in 1845, is now home to the **Sultan's Armed Forces Museum** Ⓗ (tel: +968 2431 2648; Sun–Thu 8am–1.30pm, Sat 9am–noon and 3–6pm), which gives a glimpse into Oman's military history. In the *falaj* garden are displays of tanks, armoured vehicles, aeroplanes, rockets, Exocet missiles, a navy ship and a bullet-proof Cadillac.

Ruwi proper lies across the dry wadi bed with the

### Old runway

The main street of the Central Business District running down to the Clock Tower was, amazingly, the runway of Muscat's airport until 1973. The Sultan's Armed Forces Museum inside Bait al Falaj Fort was previously at the northern end of the runway.

ONTC bus station and taxi stand at its centre. Behind the taxi stand is the modern Ruwi souq, full of electrical, optical and phone shops.

## QURM

This area is mostly made up of shopping centres and residences, but the landscape opens up around **Qurm Natural Park**, a recreational area and protected reserve of mangroves which spreads from the highway to the beach. The park is popular for family outings, with large grassy areas for picnics, playgrounds, food outlets, a lake, mock forts, and the adjoining Marah Land amusement park (tel: +968 9800 0266; www.marahland.com; open daily 3:30pm-11:30pm-midnight) and **Fun Zone** Ice Skating Center (tel: +968 9696 2422; http://funzone.om; see page 38). At the southern edge of the park, in the **Children's Museum ❶** (tel: +968 2460 5368; Sat-Wed 8am-1.30pm, Thu 9am-1pm, Oct-Mar also Mon 4-6pm), the whole family can investigate gravity, air movement, sound waves, whisper dishes, probability outcomes, the human body and many other games and puzzles. Lots of fun.

Follow Sayh al Maleh Street from the Marah Land funfair towards the PDO (Petroleum Development Oman) oil facility at Mina al Fahl and turn right just before the main entrance gate no. 2 into a small car park. The white building is the **Oil & Gas Exhibition Centre** (tel: +968 2467 7834; www.pdo.co.om; Sat-Wed 7am-noon and 1-4pm, Thu 7am-noon; free), with hands-on displays, explanations of geology, exploration, extraction and transportation, and a neighbouring **Planetarium** (tel: +968 2467 5542 one-hour shows in English every Wed; free; see page 94).

Running between the mangroves and the sandy beach, Al Shati Street (Qurm Beach Road) is a popular evening gathering place for promenading roadsters. The restaurant/coffee shops here do great business and offer stunning views towards sunset. At the eastern end is the Crowne Plaza Hotel with its small private cove and beach, overlooked by the **Ras al Hamra** headland. A walled site here shows evidence of human occupation 6,000 years ago.

Shati al Qurm continues west along the beach to the relaxed and pleasant 'Oasis by the Sea' area of shops, cafés and restaurants, some with beach views and terraces. Across the road is the Jawaharat a'Shati Complex, where the **Oman Heritage Gallery** (tel: +968 2469 6974; www.omaniheritage.com; Sat–Thu 10am–8pm) sells upmarket locally produced items on a non-profit basis. Near the Al Shati Plaza and next door to the Ramada Qurum Beach Hotel, the **Omani Society of Fine Arts** (tel: +968 2469 4969; www.osfa43.net; Sat–Wed 9.30am–1.30pm and 6–8.30pm; free) promotes art and photography appreciation.

## MADINAT AS SULTAN QABOOS

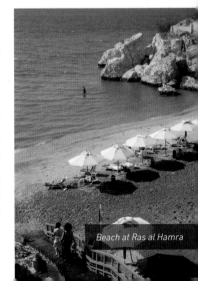

Beach at Ras al Hamra

Inland from Shati al Qurm across the main highway, the residential area of Madinat as Sultan Qaboos has two museums of interest and the sleek **Royal Opera House** ❶ (tel: +968 2440 3300; www.roh muscat.org.om; daily tours 8.30–10.30am). This fine example of Omani modern architecture is surrounded by landscaped gardens and the Opera Galleria shopping centre with numerous dining options. Follow signs to

*Traditional henna hand art*

the Ministry of Information to reach the **Omani Museum**  (tel: +968 2460 0946; Sat–Thu 8am–1.30pm), which gives an insight into traditional family life and Omani culture. The **Bait Adam Museum** (tel: +968 2460 5013; Sat–Wed 9am–1:30pm and 4–7pm), signposted off Madinat as Sultan Qaboos Street, is a remarkable private collection of photographs, coins, currency and stamps. Oman's relations with Zanzibar and the USA are revealed through important documents. Meals for small groups can be arranged directly or through any of the major tour agencies.

## AL KHUWAYR

The **Natural History Museum** (tel: 2460 4957; Sun–Thur 8am–1.30pm, Sat 9am–1pm) in Al Khuwayr is one of the most engaging museums of its size and kind anywhere, but especially welcome in a country where good background information is still hard to come by. The main attraction is a gallery of stuffed animals showing the country's diversity of wildlife. In a separate building, the Whale and Dolphin Hall exhibits skeletons found along Oman's coast, including a sperm whale suspended from the ceiling.

The highway towards the airport then passes through Bawshar roundabout to the enormous **Sultan Qaboos Grand**

**Mosque**  (tel: +968 2450 5170; www.sultanqaboosgrand mosque.com; open to non-Muslims, but no children under 12; Sat–Thu 8am–11am; free), a 'must' for all visitors and a unique opportunity to see inside an Omani mosque. This magnificent building, which opened in 2001, was constructed by the best craftsmen to celebrate the 30th anniversary of the Sultan's reign. It covers 40,000 sq metres (over 430,000 sq ft), and its main minaret rises to a height of 91.5 metres (300ft). The expansive prayer hall accommodates 6,500 worshippers below a stunning crystal chandelier and large dome, which is distinctively illuminated at night. The vast carpet, made in Iran, took over two years to make and features 28 different colours obtained from natural dyes. Visitors should wear long sleeves and trousers, and women must bring a headscarf.

*Sultan Qaboos Grand Mosque*

The opening of the huge 'Muscat City Centre' shopping mall (tel: +968 2455 8888; www.citycentremuscat.com; Sat-Wed 10am-10pm, Thur-Fri 10am-midnight) beyond the airport shows how far the city is expanding. Just after the start of the nearby road to Nizwa is the **Amouage Perfumery** (tel: +968 2453 4800; www.amouage.com; Sun–Thu 8.30am–4.30pm; free), where you can learn about perfume production and sample the varieties. Amouage perfumes, which incorporate frankincense, rosewater and myrrh, were created in the 1980s, to try to revive Oman's perfume tradition. Noted for its beautiful packaging in silver bottles plated with 24-carat gold, Amouage is one of the most expensive perfumes in the world, but the company has since launched a more affordable range. It also has an online shop. A little further on lies the **Centre for Omani Dress** (tel: +968 9891

*The glittering prayer hall of the Sultan Qaboos Grand Mosque*

9809; Mon and Wed 9.30am–12.30pm) presenting all aspects of Omani clothing.

The Muscat Expressway opened in early 2011, it runs 54km (35 miles) from Qurm to **Naseem Gardens** (Sat–Wed 4–11pm, Thu–Fri and public holidays 9am–midnight; free), a sprawling park on the way to Barka. The lakes, trees and formal gardens were opened in 1985, and a Japanese Garden was added in 2000. Together with Qurm Natural Park, it is the main focus of the annual Muscat Festival in January and February.

> **Amouage Gold**
>
> Amouage's heady signature fragrance, Gold, is often likened to the Hermès classic Calèche. Women's perfume bottles have tops shaped like a mosque dome, while men's take the form of *khanjar* daggers.

# NIZWA AND THE MOUNTAINS

Former capital of a rival imam as recently as the 1950s, Nizwa and its inhabitants have always had a different outlook to Muscat. The people here look inwards to the mountainous Ad Dakhiliyah interior and the desert, rather than outwards from the coast. The whole region is a paradise for adventure-seekers – up, down and even inside the Hajar Mountains, with the desert not far away.

## MUSCAT TO NIZWA

Beyond Muscat International Airport, the main road to Nizwa enters the mountains at Ar Rusayl. A huge area to the north of this road, around Al Khawd, will be the ambitious **Oman Botanic Garden** which will be the largest botanic garden in the Gulf region when completed. The idea is to create a sustainable

Nizwa Fort

garden reserve, featuring some 1,200 plants covering eight different environments, all accessed by 'land train'. The project is intended to be a regional and international leader in conservation.

Towards Nizwa is **Samail**, a small but neat town, its square the site of the Al Midhamr mosque, said to be the oldest in Oman. It was built in 6 AH (AD 628) by Mazin bin Ghadouba, the first Omani convert to Islam.

## NIZWA

Situated at the crossroads of ancient desert and mountain routes and blessed with a good water supply from the nearby mountains, **Nizwa ❷** became a central hub linking the remote interior with the coast. This strategic position made it wealthy through trade, and for much of its history, Nizwa has been a powerful rival to Muscat and Sohar. Today it is the most popular tourist destination outside Muscat. Most coach tours stay for just a day, but to see Nizwa properly and to visit other interesting places in the interior requires two or three days. Exiting the main highway (which continues to Jabrin and Ibri), the road into Nizwa passes most of the hotels.

The imposing 400-year-old **Nizwa Fort** (Sat–Thu 9am–4pm, Fri 9–11am) in the middle of town, has often needed to defend itself against invaders, particularly the Persians. Started in 1656 by Imam Sultan Ibn Saif Ya'arubi (who expelled the Portuguese), it was the main defensive stronghold of the town and residence of the *wali* (local governor) and his retinue. Leading from the internal courtyard is the 'Exhibits Hall', which has good explanations about local farming, the *falaj* system, crafts and a comprehensive timeline from prehistory. Climb up the impressive central tower for views over the town, market and surrounding date plantations. The outer courtyard has a small café, souvenir shop and toilets.

Just outside the main gateway is the **Omani Craftsman's House**, selling many local items. This road leads down to the tourist market of shops piled high with Bahla pots, decorated sea chests and colourful incense burners. Further along are the local markets for fruit and vegetables, meat and fish. The animal market overlooks the wadi bed, which acts as a giant car park for most of the time.

## ⊙ NIZWA LIVESTOCK MARKET

If possible, try to visit Nizwa on a Friday morning to witness the weekly animal market. The wadi car park and surrounding streets fill up from 6am as villagers arrive to sell their cows and goats. Owners walk the animals around a central ring, with potential buyers watching from both sides. A quick inspection or enquiry about an animal might lead to lengthier negotiations, conducted outside the parade ring. Dealings can get a bit heated, but generally it's all done in good spirit, and most locals seem happy for tourists to take photographs. Some of the larger cattle get a bit fed up with walking around and make an escape bid through the crowd, dragging the hapless owner with them. By 9am it is all winding down, as people drift away to buy other items at the adjacent 'car boot' sale which spreads along the wadi bed.

## AROUND NIZWA

The road to the famous forts of Bahla and Jabrin loops north along the foot of the Jabal al Akhdar Mountains. Almost immediately on the left after passing the 'Book' roundabout is a small watchtower overlooking a large plain, said to be Caliph Harun Ar Rashid's camp during his battles for regional control in the late 8th century AD. Some 20km (12 miles) from Nizwa, the next turning is for **Tanuf**, a ruined village at the entrance to a gorge. The buildings were destroyed by RAF bombers when Sultan Bin Taimur asked for Britain's aid in suppressing local support for the Imamate revolution in the 1950s. Further into the gorge is Qayut village, the departure point for some lovely mountain walks.

## AL HAMRA REGION

Thirty-five km (21 miles) from Nizwa, turn right at a roundabout towards Al Hamra and Al Hoota Cave, both well signposted. **Al Hamra** is one of the most elegant and unusual towns in the interior. It has a similar historical timescale to Nizwa, but never constructed defences and thus avoided many of the later conflicts. Curiously, for this rugged part of Oman, it has an almost Italianate feel, with terraced gardens and a piazza. Many of the grand houses are placed over *falaj* water channels running from the nearby mountains.

Immediately north of Al Hamra is a dramatic twisting road leading to the village of Misfat al Abriyyin, while the road heading west accesses **Wadi Ghul**, beyond which it climbs towards **Jabal Shams** – at 3,009 metres (9,872ft), the highest point in Oman. The summit is closed, but a track leads out onto the plateau which affords a spectacular view of **Wadi Nakhr**, known as the 'Grand Canyon', an almost vertical 1,000 metres (3,280ft) drop to the wadi below. Some of the routes into the mountains from Al Hamra are now asphalted, but generally you need a

4x4 to reach the upper mountains or penetrate the old and abandoned villages along wadi beds. Many of these 4x4 tracks now interlink eastwards and continue over the watershed to descend towards Rustaq or Al Awabi.

East of Al Hamra is the **Al Hoota Cave ❸** (tel: +968 2439 1284; www.alhootacave.com; Tue–Sun 9am–6pm, Fri 9am–noon and 2–6pm; last tours depart 5.15pm). Oman is peppered with sinkholes and caves, but this one is truly spectacular, with a forest of stalactites and stalagmites and an underground lake. Enormous effort and expense has gone into creating the walkways to access this natural cave interior without affecting the delicate ecosystem. At viewing places throughout the 45-minute visit, guides explain various aspects and facts about the cave, such as the presence of long-tailed bats, Hoota spiders and

Al Hoota Cave

## Magic fingers

It is said that the potters of Bahla are born with magic fingers. The clay they use comes from the wadi floor, but to make it soft enough to be shaped on the wheel, it must first be trampled on. When it is sufficiently pliable, the potter then works his magic, fashioning the clay into fine pots and vessels that grace homes all over Oman.

blind fish. Artificial lights illuminate the pathway and highlight the amazing calcified structures. Booking in advance is strongly advised, as numbers are limited for this popular excursion, especially at weekends.

About 4km (2.5 miles) from the cave, on the road towards Al Hamra, is a right turn signposted 'Balad Sayt 36km' and 'Al Hoota Rest House' (tel: +968 9282 2473; www.alhootaresthouse. com). Follow this asphalt road up the side of Jabal al Akhdar to reach the remote hotel after 22km (13 miles). The sealed road ends at the magnificent viewpoint of **Sharaf al Alameyn** on the central ridge at a height of exactly 2,000 metres (6,560ft) above sea level. A gravel road continues down the other side to the beautiful mountain villages of Hat and Balad Sayt set within lush palm plantations, but a 4x4 is needed to continue into the spectacular Wadi Bani Awf and exit onto the Nakhal–Rustaq road.

The small town of **Bahla**, 40km (25 miles) west of Nizwa, is dominated by an enormous fort (www.virtualbahla.com) which was in a dangerously dilapidated state when given Unesco World Heritage status in 1987. It is a fine example of a fortified oasis settlement fed by water channels, which reached the height of its importance between the 12th and 15th centuries as capital of the Bani Nebhan tribe and centre of Ibadism (see page 13). After more than 20 years, restoration is still ongoing, and it is unclear when it will reopen.

Bahla pottery is renowned throughout the region, and there are several potteries among the plantations and houses on the outskirts of town, where you can stop and watch the whole mesmerising process from treading the clay, throwing the pot (some potters still use a traditional kick wheel) and stacking the kiln to decorating.

Just 10km (6 miles) from Bahla is the splendidly isolated **Jabrin Fort ❹** (tel: +968 8007 7799 Sat–Thu 9am–4pm, Fri 9–11am), built in 1671. Despite the imposing battlements, Jabrin was not a fort but a retreat for the imams, as well as a seat of learning for students of Islamic jurisprudence, medicine and astrology. In the high-ceilinged rooms with Moghul-style arches are traces of what must have been a lavishly decorated palace. Swirling Islamic inscriptions are delicately cut into the plaster walls, and

*Bahla potter at work*

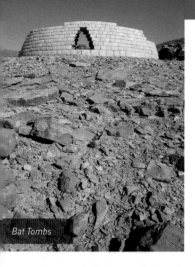
*Bat Tombs*

the wooden ceiling beams are beautifully decorated. In contrast to the splendour are the small, plain cells used by students. Below is an interesting storeroom for dates with ridged flooring that allows the dates to self-crush under their own weight into juice. Views across the open landscape from the upper towers are wonderful.

## IBRI AND BAT

Ninety km (55 miles) further west is **Ibri**, a small strategic trading town midway between Muscat and Abu Dhabi. To visit the ancient necropolis of Bat, another Unesco-listed site, turn right at the central roundabout signposted 'Diriz'. After 6km (4 miles), turn right towards Bat, immediately left at the mini roundabout, then right again towards Wahrah. Ten km (6 miles) on, turn left onto a graded track signposted 'Wadi al Ayn 23km'. After another 2km (1.2 miles), the track swings right before a fenced area, inside which lie the 4,000-year-old **Bat Tombs ❺** (always open). Some are in a better condition than others, but all originally had domed roofs. Most are constructed with an internal central wall, creating two semicircular tombs, each accessed by its own small triangular doorway. At the end of the fence across the road in a walled compound, there is a much larger communal tomb. The graded road continues 20km (12 miles) to Wadi al Ayn, where a series of remarkable stone 'beehive' tombs runs along a hill ridge.

The road between Ibri and the UAE border at Buraymi/Al Ain passes through As Sunaynah, the heart of Oman's oil industry. But to continue to Sohar, a section of road passes through the UAE, which means leaving Oman and the subsequent purchase of a new visa when re-entering.

# SOHAR AND BATINAH COAST

The Batinah coast runs from Muscat along the foot of the Western Hajar Mountains, arcing north towards the Musandam peninsula. Many wadis and natural springs keep this flat and fertile area well-watered, creating an almost continuous series of attractive ancient and modern coastal settlements. A fast dual carriageway runs parallel to the coast to Sohar, the administrative capital of the Batinah. But for an interesting detour, take the road that loops around the foot of the mountains to visit Nakhal and Rustaq forts.

## BATINAH COAST

The coast road north of Muscat passes Muscat International Airport, official gateway to Oman, and the fairly unremarkable town of Seeb, home of the Sultan Qaboos University and soon-to-be Omani aquarium, due to open in 2018. The next coastal town of significance, 80km (50 miles) from Muscat, is **Barka**. It has a fine, stout fort (Sat–Thu 8am-1pm) with a tower for panoramic views, but has become more famous for the gentle local version of **bullfighting** (bulls are pitted against bulls, but suffer little or no injury) held on Friday afternoons in the winter months. The **Barka Factory for Omani Sweets** (tel: +968 2688 2081; daily 8am-7pm) is also worth a visit to sample traditional Omani halva. Nearby is the impressive four-storey **Bait Na'aman Castle** (Sun–Thu 8am–2.30pm), featuring both round and square towers. Now fully restored and furnished, this former residence of a wealthy merchant gives a great impression of 18th-century domestic life.

The Barka roundabout on the Sohar road is also the start of the Rustaq loop, a tarmac road connecting the forts of Rustaq and Nakhal, providing many access routes into dramatic mountain gorges for exciting treks and off-road driving in a 4x4.

Crowning a spur at the wadi's head, some 32km (20 miles) from the Sohar road, the awesome **Nakhal Fort** ⑥ (Sat–Thu 9am-5pm) is certainly a major highlight. Soaring to a height of 30 metres (98ft) above ground level, its foundations are believed to pre-date Islam, though the fort itself has been remodelled many times since. Nakhal was entirely self-contained, with well-water and storage rooms for stockpiling in the event of a siege. The *wali* (governor) lived on the mezzanine level in winter and on the breezy upper terrace during the hot summer months. His *majlis* (audience room) is lined with hand-woven carpets, and the harem is spread with carpets and cushions. A sweeping panorama of the plantations and mountains can be enjoyed from the top of the fort.

*Ancient inscriptions decorate the ceiling of Nakhal Fort*

The 52km (32-mile) road to Rustaq passes the entrances to several spectacular gorges, such as Wadi Sabt (to access Wadi Mistall and the Gubrah Bowl), Wadi Bani Kharus

*A Batinah coast beach resort*

(for Wuqan village and the Sayl Plateau) and Wadi Bani Awf (for the trek through the heart of Jabal Akhdar to the tarmac road above Al Hoota Rest House, see page 137). Fortresses protect these access routes, including Al Awabi and **Rustaq Fort** (Sat–Thu 8am–4pm, Fri 8am–11am). The biggest fortification in Oman after Bahla, it is built over the site of a spring which gushes around its base. The four huge towers typify Omani defensive architecture. Rustaq's lush date plantations are watered by more than 200 *falaj*, but bursting out of the limestone, about a mile from the town centre, is Ain al Kasfah, a hot spring said to have healing powers. Halfway between Rustaq and rejoining the Sohar road is **Al Hazm Fort** (Sat–Thu 7am–4pm, Fri 7am–11am), beautifully set amongst palms and *falaj* water channels.

The Rustaq loop rejoins the Sohar road near Al Musanaah. Between Al Musanaah and Barka is **Ras as Sawadi**, a headland with several offshore islands, the nesting ground for thousands

Sohar Fort

of migratory birds. It is a popular site for hiring local boats on late afternoons and at weekends. The spacious As Sawadi Beach Resort (al-sawadi-beach-resort.muscat-hotels-om.com) offers watersports, including diving, and horse- and camel-riding.

The coast from here to Sohar is dotted with coastal towns, each with its own fort or castle, the pick of them being the seldom-visited **As Suwayq** (Sun–Thu 8.30am–2.30pm), one of the best 'coastal-style' defences. It is worthwhile exploring these smaller towns with their compact harbours and beach-side fish markets for a taste of local life.

## SOHAR

**Sohar** ❼, the Batinah capital, is a pleasant, prosperous town with clean streets lined with white houses and tropical gardens. For millennia it was the major port and capital of an ancient kingdom known as Magan, which became wealthy through the production and trade of copper from the inland mountains. One of its earliest trading partners was the Mesopotamian city of Ur at the other end of the Arabian Gulf. The fabulous Emporium Persicum near the Strait of Hormuz mentioned in a 5th-century Byzantine text is almost certainly Sohar, home port of Sindbad the Sailor of the *Thousand and One Nights*. Sohar reached its zenith in the 10th century, when it thrived on trade with Africa and Madagascar. The seaport was absorbed into the Persian kingdom of Hormuz in the 14th century, but following capture by Portugal in 1507 its fortunes began to ebb. By the mid-16th century, shipping from India and Africa discharged in Sur and Aden and local merchants and sea captains moved elsewhere.

Sohar's fortunes have recently revived, thanks to the development of a major new port, factories and oil refineries, making it second only to Muscat in terms of economic importance. The town has an extensive seafront corniche ending at the harbour and the sweeping roof of the new fish market, and new malls now complement the more traditional souqs. The large, whitewashed **Sohar Fort** (Sat–Thu 9am–4pm, Fri 8–11am) at the eastern end of the corniche is the main attraction. A

## ⦿ SINDBAD THE SAILOR

Sindbad is one of the main protagonists of the nightly stories spun out by legendary Persian queen Scheherazade to save her own neck, as told in the book of *One Thousand and One Nights*. Although fictional, the tales are based on the real-life adventures recounted and embellished by merchants and seamen for hundreds of years. According to these fantastical stories involving monsters, magic and flights of fancy, Sindbad embarks on a series of voyages, all of which go disastrously wrong. But through cunning and skill, not only does he escape with his life, but he also returns with great wealth...until his next voyage. Although there are many other claims, all Omanis believe that Sindbad originally came from Sohar. His name would appear to have a connection with Sindh (now in Pakistan) with which Sohar was trading. Sindbad's voyage to China was recreated by Tim Severin in a replica craft named *Sohar* (see page 59).

Flooded waste pit in the arid Sohar hinterland, where copper has been mined for millennia

fortress has probably been on this site for over 1,500 years, but most of what is seen today dates from the Portuguese period in the early16th century. Further north are the Sohar Beach Hotel (tel: 968-2684 1111; www.soharbeach.com) and the Butterfly Hotel Suites (tel: +968 2684 3501; www.butterflyoman.com).

Continuing along the main coastal highway is Shinas, where most of the traffic turns inland on the main road to Dubai, with the border control at Hatta. North along the coast road is the border with Fujairah emirate at Khitmat Milahah, 90km (55 miles) from Sohar.

## WADI JIZZI

The road between Sohar and Buraymi runs inland up **Wadi Jizzi**, a thoroughfare between the mountains used for thousands of years to transport extracted minerals, particularly copper. There are two sites of interest both connected with the ancient copper trade – a ziggurat temple and the Lusayl Arch, both reachable by car.

Three km (2 miles) after leaving the Falaj al Qubail roundabout on the outskirts of Sohar, the Crowne Plaza Hotel is seen on the right. The great belching smokestack of the modern Oman Mining processing plant, 25km (15 miles) on, is always a good location marker when exploring the area. To reach the ziggurat, turn right off the Buraymi road in front of the Oman Mining gates and double back up what appears to be a private road into the copper plant. Follow this public tarmac road between the two halves of the mining plant. After 5km (3 miles) you'll be glad to know that you are not going into Rehab (signposted left) as you take the road fork 1,500 metres/yds to a fenced area on the left with 'Keep Out' signs, inside which is a huge open-cast mine known as 'Beidha Pit', now disused. Just over a kilometre (0.6 miles) further on is a signpost indicating Beidha village to the left, and here on the right, beside the road, are the stone ramps and tiers of the ziggurat.

The small **Arja Ziggurat** ❽, the only such temple yet found in Arabia, reveals the ancient connections with Persia and Mesopotamia, where ziggurats are more common. Many ancient copper-smelting sites have been discovered in the area, some dating back 4,000 years, and it is likely that Sumerian gods would have

### Ziggurats

Ziggurats were stepped pyramid temples built from about 2,200 BC to 500 BC in the Gulf region, of which about 25 survive. The best preserved is at Ur in Iraq, while the largest is at Elam in Iran. Nobody knows for certain how or why these vast temples were built, but it is thought that they were designed as dwelling places for the gods rather than places of worship.

The Lusayl Arch

been worshipped at such a temple. Shaped like a step pyramid with an access ramp up one side, this temple probably had four tiers, of which only the lower two remain. Dating is difficult, but it could be from around 1,000 BC.

The **Lusayl Arch** is on the other side of the Buraymi Road, reached by returning to the Oman Mining plant and continuing towards Buraymi. Two km (1.2 miles) after the plant, take the slip road signposted 'Sehaylah al Sharqiyah'. Turn left under the road, signposted 'Oman Mining/Sohar' as if returning back towards Sohar, and instead of rejoining the main road, turn right at the end of the crash barriers onto an old potholed tarmac road. Pass the small labourers' camp of Oman Abrasives on the left and cross a wadi bed as the road becomes a gravel track, but still good enough for non- 4x4 cars. Enter a large clearing with an abandoned, fenced mine opening on the right. Park here and walk between the dead palm trees on the left and an abandoned white building on the right. Pass the multicoloured flooded waste pits on the left, keeping away from the crumbling and overhanging edges. The Lusayl Arch is 200 metres/yds ahead on the right. Quite why this small natural arch has been chosen to promote Oman's tourism industry is a mystery. It is pleasant enough, but hardly a major attraction.

The main road continues to Buraymi, an oasis town of three villages, but greatly undeveloped compared with its six neighbouring villages that now constitute Al Ain, lying within Abu Dhabi emirate. It is possible to visit Buraymi, observe Jabal Hafit and drive south towards the oilfields around As Sunaynah and on to Ibri and Nizwa; however, as the border post is several kilometres before Buraymi, this involves the cancellation of your current visa and the purchase of another one to get back into Oman. This is regardless of whether you travel onto Nizwa or return to Sohar from Buraymi.

## SUR AND THE EAST

One of the most varied regions of the country is the coastal strip between Muscat and Ras al Hadd, the most easterly point in Arabia. Between the desert and the rugged coast around Sur is a range of dramatic mountains, indented with voluminous caves, jagged sinkholes and weathered wadis. The main coastal towns on this stretch are Qurayyat, an important fishing community, and Sur, a historic boatbuilding and trading centre. A two-day circuit runs inland from the east coast back to Muscat through numerous towns along the edge of the spectacular Wahibah sand sea, from where excursions can be taken into the desert.

### MUSCAT TO SUR

The modern road from Muscat leaves Ruwi and runs through some narrow gorges before passing Al Amrat and its stargazing

The Bimmah Sinkhole

observation site, exactly on the Tropic of Cancer. Another 30km (18 miles) on, the road skirts the **Wadi Sireen Reserve**, set up to protect the Arabian tahr, a rare breed of mountain goat indigenous to the Hajar Mountains. The road reaches the coast at **Qurayyat**, a town of mangrove swamps, but now being pleasantly developed. The modern coastal highway then slices along the cliffs with many access points into the mountains, the easiest being Wadi al Arbiyeen, some 5km (3 miles) after the toll-booths. Eight km (5 miles) later is a sign to Dibab and the Hawryat Najm Park, where the **Bimmah Sinkhole ❾** (open daily 8am-11pm) is located. One of several in Oman, the hole is about 70 metres (230ft) wide and 30 metres (98ft) deep. It was created when the limestone roof of a cave collapsed. There are changing rooms if you wish to put on your swimming costume and clamber down for a cooling dip in the blue-green water. In the mountains above lies **Majlis al Jinn** ('meeting place of spirits'), it is the second largest known natural cave chamber in the world.

Beyond the popular camping spot of Fins Beach is the town of **Tiwi ❿**, sandwiched between two dramatic wadis. The first, **Wadi Shab**, offers a great two-hour return walk. A local boat carries walkers across a stretch of water to the start of the walk, which passes through plantations and canyons (you may have to wade through some water, depending on water levels). **Wadi Tiwi**, on the other side of the town, is quite different, as 4x4 vehicles can drive more than 7km (4 miles) along it to the small hamlet of Mibam, beyond which is further easy trekking. The more adventurous can arrange to camp overnight and climb over the mountains to drop into Wadi Bani Khalid on the other side.

A little further down the coast is the once great port of **Qalhat**, famous for the mausoleum of Bibi Maryam (believed to date from the 13th-century). When Muslim explorer Ibn Battuta came here in the 14th century he described a city thriving on the trade of horses, but the ancient city was subsequently destroyed by an

## ⊙ RECREATING SINDBAD'S VOYAGE

The adventures of Sindbad as recounted in the *One Thousand and One Nights* are almost certainly based on real accounts of ancient Omani mariners. At least 3,000 years ago the monsoon winds allowed them to trade copper and incense beyond India to the Far East. On the way back they carried silk, spices, precious stones, gold and porcelain. Irish adventurer Tim Severin wanted to recreate such epic sea journeys to China, and oversaw the construction of a typical 9th-century boat, built with wooden planks sewn together by coconut-fibre rope. Severin chose the boatbuilding town of Sur to get this type of *boom* constructed in just seven months by a specialist team. The name *Sohar* was chosen, as most Omanis believe that to be the birthplace of Sindbad. On 21 November 1980 Severin's team set sail across the Indian Ocean using 1,000-year-old technology and night stars for navigation. They sailed the maritime silk route past India, Sri Lanka, Sumatra and Malaysia to arrive in Canton less than eight months later.

earthquake and then by Portuguese invaders. Note that some coastal towns are only accessible from the new highway when travelling from the Sur direction. The road into Sur now runs inland past the large liquid natural gas complex run by Oman LNG.

## SUR

From Qalhat, the road descends to the port of **Sur ⑪**. Famous for its great tradition of boatbuilding, it was a major trading port with East Africa, especially Zanzibar, during the 18th and 19th centuries, but its prosperity declined after slavery was abolished. The **Sunaysilah Castle** (Sun–Thu 7am–6pm;) is over 300 years old. Sitting on a low hill, it offers extensive views over the modern town (the best views are from the western tower, accessed via a wooden rung ladder). The crumbling Old Town is located on a spit of land that is almost an island at the entrance to the shallow lagoon, with the adjoining town of Al Ayjah on the other side. The views across the end of the lagoon towards a line of whitewashed houses, light-house, mosque and moored dhows are breathtaking.

The main sights here are the nearby **boatyards**, with new wooden craft at various stages of completion and the **Maritime Museum**. Exhibits are still being moved here from the old museum collection near Sunaysilah Castle, but some full-sized boats are on display, including *Fatah al Khair*. This restored ocean-going passenger dhow, known as a *ghanjah*, was one of the last of its kind to be built in Sur about 70 years ago. The Al Ayjah road bridge towards Ras al Hadd crosses the entrance of the lagoon but is only for smaller vehicles.

It is 34km (21 miles) from Al Ayjah Bridge to a T-junction sign-posting Ras al Hadd to the left and Ras al Jinz to the right. Four km (2.5 miles) after turning left is a small roundabout, approaching Ras al Hadd. Turn left here for the 7km (4-mile) winding road to Turtle Beach Resort nestled on the edge of Khawr al Hajar

*The endangered green turtle at Ras Al Jinz Turtle Reserve*

lagoon; otherwise continue straight ahead to drive around the other side of the lagoon. The 450-year-old Ras al Hadd Castle is on the left after 6km (3.5 miles), and Resort Ras al Hadd Holiday is further on. Between the castle and the hotel are the two runways of the disused RAF base on the expanse of ground to the right.

## TURTLE-WATCHING

Witnessing the remarkable spectacle of female turtles laying their eggs in the sand south of Ras al Hadd has become one of the highlights for many visitors to Oman. More turtles arrive on the beaches each night during the main laying season between July and October, but they can turn up on any night of the year. There is nothing to stop anyone simply spending the night along any of the beaches outside the Ras al Jinz reserve in the hope of seeing a turtle. But as these green turtles *(Chelonia mydas)* are an endangered species, the whole idea of the turtle reserve is to protect

Turtle tracks in the sand

them from human interference and allow them to lay their eggs in peace. Egg-laying and hatching turtles are only seen at night.

The **Ras al Jinz Turtle Reserve 12** (tel: +968 9655 0606/0707; www.rasaljinz-turtlereserve.com) was established by royal decree in 1996 and is committed to protecting the sea turtles and their natural environment, and the beach visits are responsibly managed. They are conducted twice nightly: groups of 30 assemble at the reserve to be guided to the beach at 9pm (for the egg-laying) and at 4.30am (for the hatching of baby turtles). Strict guidelines control these visits – smoking, mobile phones and photography are forbidden. Flashlights can be used to get to the beach, but must be switched off near the turtles. When the guides find a turtle, smaller groups are invited to approach and observe the egg-laying process by low-light torches. From a safe distance the group waits for the turtle to cover the eggs with her flippers. During the wait, the guide explains the life-cycle of the turtles, giving facts and figures. As a bonus for evening visitors, some previously hatched baby turtles might be released to make their way clumsily into the sea. Around 3,500 visitors a month visit the centre, so reservations are essential and can be made up to 12 months ahead. The beach is also open daily for paying visitors from 8am to 1.30pm to observe turtle tracks in the sand, but it is unusual for turtles to be seen in daytime.

As for accommodation, the easiest option is to stay at the reserve centre itself, but there are only 31 rooms which are booked far ahead. Four km (2.5 miles) inland from the reserve is the Al Naseem Camp, a tented site similar to the more distant Turtle Beach Resort, 22km (13 miles) away. Despite the name, there are no turtles at Turtle Beach Resort, which has a series of wooden cabins set back from the beach of a lagoon, opposite the Resort Ras al Hadd Holiday. Some reserve visitors stay at the hotels in Sur, requiring night drives of at least 45 minutes each way.

## THE EASTERN HAJAR MOUNTAINS

A circuit of the Eastern Hajar Mountains runs inland from Al Ashkharah and returns to Muscat via Al Kamil, Ibra and Bidbid. Just outside Al Kamil on the inland road to Sur is the As Saleel Nature Park, forested with acacia trees and home to Arabian gazelles and the Omani wild cat. **Wadi Bani Khalid** is an easily accessible series of natural pools which have been popular with both locals and tourists for many years, especially at weekends and holidays. It is a 10-minute walk from the car park up a paved path to reach the pools. Local children will carry heavy picnic hampers in wheelbarrows for a small fee.

**Ibra** is a modern town with a general souq, but more interesting is the women's souq held on a Wednesday from 8am until noon. On this day, men are banned from

> ### Turtle facts
>
> A female green turtle always lays her eggs – up to 100 at a time – on the beach where she herself hatched out. In her 70-or-so-year lifespan, she might return here to nest three times. Only two or three out of every 1,000 turtles born actually survive to maturity. Those that make it to the water will never see their mother again.

trading and the tradeswomen sell bolts of silk and satin brocades, jewellery, sandalwood, kitchen goods, spices and produce.

Just south of Ibra lies the old ruined trading town of **Al Minzafah**, reached by turning left in the centre of town and then right at the end of a long wall, below the first watchtower. This crumbling collection of mud and stone houses, shops, caravanserais and mosques is wonderful to look around.

## WAHIBAH DESERT AND BEYOND

Sunset and sunrise provide spectacular photo opportunities of the unique **Wahibah Desert**. Strung along the edge of the orange-coloured sand dunes are the towns of Adam, Sinaw, Al Mudaybi, Bidiyyah and Al Mintirib. **Bidiyyah** has a small private museum (tel: +968 9935 0757; Sat–Thur 9am–12pm, 2–6pm)

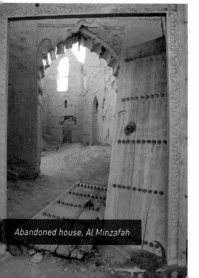

*Abandoned house, Al Minzafah*

focusing on desert traditions, and **Al Mintirib** has a fort (Sun–Thu 7:30am–2:30pm). Many tour agencies have camps nearby (see page 123), from where they organise 4x4 (and sometimes camel) safaris into the dunes, with at least one night spent camping amid the silent expanse of sand and stars.

Knowledgeable desert guides can lead vehicles through the Wahibah Desert to the coast at Barr al Hikman and Shanna, for the regular ferry across to

**Masirah Island** ⓭, where many of the beaches are also favoured by nesting turtles, mainly loggerheads. Shanna can also be reached on a good, fast road from Muscat in about five hours. The ferry leaves when full and operates a few times through the day; it charges per vehicle, not per passenger. Coral reefs, shipwrecks, marine and birdlife, and one of the best windsurfing sites in the world are among the many reasons to visit Masirah, a wonderfully remote island of beaches, perfect for camping. The one classy hotel and two local ones will soon be joined by many others as there is an on-going plan to construct a 25km (16-mile) causeway bridge linking Masirah with the mainland.

Back on the mainland, a long coastal route runs south towards Salalah through Duqm, set to become a desert and wildlife tourist hub upon completion of the new airport. Inland from Duqm is the **Jiddat al Harasis** region and its **Arabian Oryx Sanctuary**, established in 1974. A permit is required for a visit, but poaching and increased oil exploration in the area has seen oryx numbers decline, and they are now kept safe in much smaller fenced areas.

## SALALAH AND DHOFAR

Dhofar, Oman's southern province, is a ruggedly beautiful region with a rich history rooted in the ancient frankincense trade. Cut off from the rest of the country by the southeastern corner of the Empty Quarter desert, it shares a border with Yemen to the south and in the north melts into the gravel plains of the Jiddat al Harasis. Its mountains attract the *khareef* (southwest monsoon) blowing off the Indian Ocean, and, unusually, the busiest season is mid-summer, as visitors come here to enjoy the cooling rains, when the rest of the country is paralysingly hot. Lush woodland is sustained by the rainfall, and along the

An unspoilt beach in Dhofar

luxuriant coastline coconut trees bend over pure white beaches. Sightseeing of the region can only be done by arranging a local tour, hiring a taxi for the day or renting a car.

## SALALAH CITY

Most people travel to Dhofar by air, a spectacular 90-minute flight across the Wahibah Sands from Muscat. On the approach to **Salalah** ⑭ the brown terrain is flecked with green, and the drop down onto the coastal plain is sudden and exciting. The airport is near to the centre, reached by a connecting road to the 'clock tower' roundabout, overlooked by the Haffa House Hotel (tel: +968 232 95444; www.shanfarihotels.com/hotel/haffa-house-salalah.php). Immediately behind the Haffa House Hotel on Al Matar Street is a remarkable site within a small, well-tended garden, signposted as the **Mausoleum of Nabi Umran**. Inside a long building is the tomb of this pre-Islamic prophet, almost 40 metres (130ft) in length, adorned by bright rugs and bouquets of flowers. Further down Al Matar Street is the beautiful **Wazir Shanfari Mosque**, built in 1995.

The centre of the modern city is set around the junction of 23rd July Street and An Nahdah Street, surrounded by regional government buildings and the Sultan Qaboos Mosque. The continuation of An Nahdah Street runs past the gold and silver souq to the Palace of Sultan Qaboos, known as Al Hosn.

Though out of bounds, it is a useful marker for getting to the **Alafa Souq** just to the east. All tourist groups are brought here to buy frankincense at a series of shops, each burning small amounts of the aromatic gum resin.

Salalah lies on a superb beach extending 39km (24 miles) east to Taqah. The corniche runs for 3km (2 miles) to the Al Balid district and is a wonderful place to visit towards sunset, when the locals promenade along the seafront or chat in groups at the many local cafés and restaurants.

One of the most important recent developments is the uncovering of the **Al Balid archaeological site** of ancient Salalah. Known as Zafar, it was visited by the 14th-century traveller Ibn Battuta, who noted its many mosques and observed that its people traded in frankincense, horses and fish-oil with merchants from India. This large site of excavated buildings amidst tranquil canals and lagoons is also home to the new and impressive **Land of Frankincense Museum** (Sun–Wed 8am– 2pm and 4–8pm, Thu–Fri 4–8pm; no photography inside). The two indoor sections lead from a courtyard with a fine specimen of a frankincense tree at its centre. The History Hall covers pre-history, frankincense, geography, Islam and modern Oman

Mausoleum of Nabi Umran

and provides a real insight into the people of the region. The Maritime Hall concentrates on boatbuilding, seamanship, navigation and the trade that made the region wealthy.

Salalah is ringed by mountains. Rain falling on these highlands during the summer *khareef* is soaked up and stored in layers of limestone. As well as the great caverns that open up to create sinkholes such as Tawi Atayr, the water is also slowly released throughout the year at a series of springs along the base of the mountains. Known as *ains*, these springs are pleasant spots, all within a 15-minute drive of the coast. The easiest to reach is **Ain Razat**, but Ain Jarziz, Ain Hamran, Ain Tabraq and Ain Athun are all popular evening and weekend retreats. The abundance of open water and vegetation also attracts varied birdlife.

*Frankincense tree*

## WEST SALALAH

Camels grazing at Ain Razat

The main road heading into the mountains from the western end of the ring road behind the Hamdan Plaza Hotel (tel: +968 2321 1024; www.hamdan plazahotel.com) is known as the Atin Road. Each side of the road has large areas used during the *khareef* – amusement parks, campsites, and picnic and play areas. Beyond the outer ring road the road climbs into the mountains. Halfway up, a broken cobbled road doubles back on the right to a viewpoint, known as the Atin Cave restaurant. The views across Salalah and the coast are fabulous, especially at sunset. The shallow **Atin Cave** itself is along a paved walkway behind the restaurant, offering great views into the neighbouring wooded valley. Ten km (6 miles) beyond Atin Cave is the sign-posted 'Mausoleum of An Nabi Ayoub' (**Job's Tomb**), another pre-Islamic prophet whose grave is about 4 metres (13ft) long. Famed in the Old Testament for maintaining his faith in God in spite of the sufferings sent to test him, Job (Ayoub in Arabic) is revered by Muslims as well as Jews and Christians.

Return to the Hamdan Plaza roundabout, turn right and head towards the western suburbs and port area. The Sumhuram Tourist Village and Hilton Resort are along the coast to the left. Eight km (5 miles) after passing the **Port of Salalah** at Raysut, where cruise ships dock, some fenced compounds display rows of young frankincense trees. The road then crosses a moonscape desert before dropping down to **Mughsayl Beach**, where white sand stretches to the distant cliffs, edged by more fenced trees – this time coconuts, providing welcome shade for visitors. After the fishing village (a row of smart villas to the right of the road) is an inlet. As the road starts to climb (and opposite a petrol station on the right), turn left, signposted 'Al Marneef Cave'. The cliff path ends at some wooden platforms overlooking the crashing sea, where pummelling seawater has undermined the edges, creating chambers and **blow holes** within the rocks. Hope for rough seas, as the water is forced through small passageways and explodes spectacularly upwards out of the ground. In calm weather, nothing happens apart from a few gurgling noises deep underground.

Mughsayl Beach is known for giant blow holes

It is worthwhile continuing further west on the main road, as just over 7km (4 miles) from the petrol station are some wild frankincense trees, just to the right of the road at the bottom of steep downhill bends. These are scraggy specimens which have been well attacked by visitors wishing to draw out the precious white sap. Some hardened beads of aromatic resin might be found on the old, gnarled barks. Even the slivers of wood and bark smell of the wonderful fragrance. Further still are some dramatic views from the mountain road as it snakes up the coastal cliffs, with a few parking places to stop and view. The area of Thaytiniti is rich in fossils of large mammals that used to roam here.

### Wilfred Thesiger

The great British adventurer made two epic camel rides across the Empty Quarter desert in the 1940s, the first starting in Dhofar. Travelling with Omani tribesmen, his accounts are told in one of the greatest travel books of all time, *Arabian Sands*.

## EAST SALALAH

Heading east out of Salalah, there are several turn-offs leading to more *ains* at the foot of the mountains, before turning right for **Taqah** ⑮, 36km (22 miles) from Salalah. The town has a thriving fishing industry along the beach, but the main interest is the restored stronghold in the middle of town. **Taqah Fort** (Sat–Thu 9am–4pm, Fri 8–11am), at the entrance to the Old Town, is a fine example of coastal fort architecture, with rooms wonderfully decorated in period style. Behind the fine carved wooden doors, exhibitions of Dhofari lifestyle, culture and history are well explained in English and Arabic. The views from the top of any of the three square defensive towers are tremendous. The Women's Handicraft shop to the left of the entrance is well worth visiting, with a wide selection of silver rings, bracelets, basketware, incense burners, clothes and hats, mostly made by local women. Just behind the fort, up a steep flight of steps is a smaller 200-year-old fort with even better views across the town.

The road inland from Taqah, signposted 'Tawi Atayr' and 'Taiq', leads to two sites of interest. **Wadi Darbat**, to the left,

Taqah Fort

is an area of dense vegetation, camel-grazing and natural caves that really only comes alive during the *khareef* rains, when the waters of the wadi turn into waterfalls that cascade down the valley. The transformation makes it a popular picnic spot in summer. To the right and up into the mountains, the road eventually leads to **Tawi Atayr** (signposted 'Atair Sinkhole'), a large limestone cave with the collapsed roof now lying at the bottom of a huge chasm.

Five km (3 miles) east of Taqah is the entrance to some of Oman's most important historical remains – the Unesco World Heritage Site of **Sumhuram** ⑯ (www.omanwhs.gov.om/English/Frank/khorroricomplex.asp; Sat–Fri 8am–7pm; entry charge per vehicle), once the principal port for the export of frankincense. The trading centre prospered for over 1,000 years, thanks largely to the monsoon winds which blew the heavily laden trading boats towards Yemen and the Red Sea. The site is entered through an impressive gateway with some wall blocks inscribed in Sabaean (South Arabian) text. Inside are extensive walled buildings variously identified as a palace, temple, living areas and storage rooms.

Excavated Sumhuram sits on top of a hill overlooking the silted-up natural inlet of **Khawr Rawri**. Once the mouth of the harbour, it is now a freshwater creek, separated from the sea by a sandbank which attracts many migratory bird species, including pelican, stork, spoonbill and flamingo. You can drive or walk to the coast about 2km (1.2 miles) away by taking the track past the **Archaeological Gallery** (same timings as the site; free). This small collection has been superseded by the new Land of Frankincense Museum in Salalah but has some interesting site finds, showing influences from Marib, the capital of Sheba (in Yemen), and Mesopotamia.

Yemen has also influenced Dhofar's modern history, as it was the overspill from the successful campaigns to oust the British from Aden in the 1960s that led to the Dhofar campaign against the ruling Sultan in Muscat. To defeat the rebels, the Sultan called upon British troops and in particular

## ⊙ THE FRANKINCESE TRADE

Trade in these precious aromatic tree resins, burnt as fumigants, has been in existence for more than 3,000 years. Writing in the 5th century BC, the historian Herodotus tells us that 'Arabia is the only country which produces frankincense and myrrh' to be used extensively by ancient Egyptian priests in temples along the Nile as offerings to the gods. The dried sap from these Dhofar trees was originally carried by ships along the coast to Yemen, where they were repackaged and sent off on the great overland trade route through the Queen of Sheba's territory. Myrrh is a similar but smaller shrub, whose resin was used in the process of mummification. Fragmentation of the South Arabian tribes, the rise of Christianity and the emergence of the overland Silk Road all led to the demise of this once great trade.

the SAS, in exchange for his continued co-operation with British oil companies. The coastal town of **Mirbat** ⑰ further east saw most of the military action, when British forces were often based at the fort which overlooks the town and harbour. To the west of Mirbat is the twin onion-domed white mausoleum of the prophet Bin Ali, set in the corner of a vast Muslim cemetery. His 5-metre (16ft) -long tomb is draped in canopies of green silk.

East of Mirbat is the Marriott Beach Hotel. Some time ago the dive centre discovered the wreck of an old steamship about 1,000 metres (3,280ft) offshore. Running parallel to the coast between Mirbat and Hasik is Jabal Samhan, a nature reserve concerned with the protection of the Arabian leopard and Nubian ibex.

Girl at Mirbat

On the main desert road linking Dhofar with Nizwa and 77km (48 miles) inland from Salalah is the desert town of **Thumrayt**, with its large air force base, a survival post on the edge of the Empty Quarter. The ancient city of **Ubar** is said to be located at Shisr, a further 70km (40 miles) north, through a featureless landscape and only reachable by 4x4. These ruins and many others show that large frankincense-trading towns existed in Dhofar throughout the 1st millennium BC.

*Stunning views of Khawr Sham on a Musandam dhow cruise*

# MUSANDAM

With spectacular mountains plunging into turquoise waters, rocky bays and isolated fishing villages, Musandam is one of the great secrets of Arabia, reckoned by many to be the most beautiful region in Oman. Exploring any part of this remote and rugged peninsula, cut off from the rest of country by part of the UAE, is an adventure whether by land or by sea. Dolphins follow the dhows as they meander through the fjord-like inlets, while eagle-eyed raptors watch the 4x4s as they inch their way up the tortuous mountain bends to see high plateaus, stone houses and ancient rock carvings. Until the early 1990s, the peninsula was a strictly military zone. However, as Oman has gradually opened up to tourism, so has the Musandam, and it has become a popular weekend destination for visitors based in Dubai and Abu Dhabi, just a few hours' drive away.

## GETTING TO MUSANDAM

Getting to the peninsula is an adventure in itself. The easiest and quickest way is to take the hour-long flight on a turbo-prop from Muscat, which affords spectacular views over the mountains and coast. Slower and less reliable is the twice-weekly ferry. The journey from Muscat to Khasab takes over five hours, but these sailings are sometimes cancelled through the winter months due to rough seas. Driving to Musandam is also an option, but with parts of the UAE in between, all paperwork (including a road pass issued by the Royal Oman Police) and insurance must be pre-arranged. New Oman visas are required for tourists entering Musandam by road and then re-entering Oman on the way back, but are not required if arriving by plane or ferry from Muscat. A departure tax from the UAE might also need to be paid in Dirhams. Some of the minor roads can get washed away in the heavy rains of January and February.

## KHASAB

The provincial capital, **Khasab** ⑱, is a quiet, pleasant town stretching back through palm plantations from the broad harbour 5km (3 miles) up the valley to the airport. Overlooking the seafront is the restored **Khasab Fort** (Sat–Thu 9am–4pm, Fri 8–11am), a splendid stronghold built by the Portuguese in the 17th century. It now houses an ethnographic museum, full of fascinating insights into the lifestyles of

### Iranian smugglers

The coast of Iran can be reached in under an hour by fast speedboat from Khasab. Every night hundreds of smugglers load their tiny boats with electronic goods bought in Khasab souq to run the gauntlet of Iranian patrols and supertankers as they race across the Strait of Hormuz.

*Zaruqah boat decorated with cowrie shells, Khasab Fort*

the tribes that have made Musandam their home. There are interesting exhibits on geological history, fishing techniques and early trade routes, plus a display of traditional Omani boats. This region is the last place in Arabia still to use wooden planks, sewn together with palm-fibre rope in the process of building *battil* and *zaruqah* boats.

Not far away, in the narrow alleys of the wealthy suburb of Al Wusta, is another small fort. **Al Khmazera Fort** (Sat–Wed 8am–2pm) has a fully functioning well in the middle of its courtyard and wonderful views from its roof terrace across the plantations and mosque. The main centre of Khasab is set around the new mosque with a limited choice of shops and restaurants.

## SCENIC COASTAL DRIVE

The spectacular coast road from Khasab down the north-west coast to Bukha rates as one of the best in Oman. Running

*Snorkelling stop-off on a dhow cruise*

parallel with the sea, the road is blasted through the feet of mountains, revealing vivid bands of marbling. Follow the main road west out of Khasab beyond Bassa Beach and the Atana Khasab Hotel and head for **Qada Bay**, a spectacular place known for its petroglyphs (engravings pecked into the rocks). Turn left at the head of the inlet to go through Qada village, always keeping to the left side of the wadi. Just after a large white government building, the tarmac ends. Keep going along the gravel road for another 1km (0.6 miles) to the small settlement of Tawi, surrounded by towering, weathered cliff faces. When the track turns sharp right around an open water pool shaded by three trees, and just before the gorge splits into two, look at the jumble of fallen rocks on the left side. Some of these feature ancient carvings of men riding camels and horses. The location alone is worth the journey. There are abandoned villages on the mountain-tops on both sides of this wadi.

Bukha lies on the Gulf coast side of Musandam. The eastern side of the town contains **Bukha Fort** (Sat–Thu 9am–4pm, Fri 8–11am; free), which looks different from most Omani forts because of its distinctive pear-shaped tower designed for deflecting cannonballs.

From Bukha to the UAE border at Ras al Khaimah is just a 30-minute drive.

# DHOW CRUISE

The most popular excursion in Musandam is to take a dhow cruise and explore the inlets and bays that punctuate the coastline, often accompanied by dolphins. All hotels and tour agencies offer dhow excursions, catering for between five and 20 passengers. The usual day cruise is spent sailing around the dramatic 20km (12-mile) -long **Khawr Sham** fjord to the east of Khasab. The layers of folded rock and geological formations are stunning. With stops for snorkelling at Telegraph Island and Seebi Island, even a novice swimmer can enjoy viewing the colourful fish in completely calm and safe waters, as colourful wrasse and sergeant-majors flit between the more ponderous angel and parrot fish. To protect the local people from too much intrusion, all of the tiny fishing settlements are out of bounds for tourists. Lunch is often a barbecue cooked on board by one of the crew.

The only way to visit the more remote coastal settlements such as Kumzar and Musandam's east coast is to arrange a longer cruise, lasting between two and four days, either camping on the beach or sleeping on the deck of the dhow. Several tour companies offer this as part of their itineraries (see page 122). **Kumzar village** is tucked between huge mountain walls. The houses are strung along the lower slopes and look towards Iran, from where the unique language spoken by the villagers originates.

Sailing around the end of the peninsula can be

### Telegraph Island

This small island became famous as an unpopular posting for British engineers who were laying the first telegraph line between Britain and India. It is said that the expression 'going round the bend' was used to describe the location and boredom.

dangerous because of the strong currents. The constant flow of water into the gulf reduces visibility, but the rich nutrients support a wealth of marine creatures such as whale sharks, eagle rays and even pods of orcas. Most scuba-dives are 'drift dives' and generally not for the novice. As the only permitted dive operator, the Extra Divers team based at the Atana Khasab Hotel can best monitor and control the diving activity around this pristine marine area.

## MOUNTAIN TOUR

Having seen the mountains from the tranquillity of the inlets at sea level, the next step is to venture into them for sweeping vistas across this spectacular landscape from on high. The sensible way is to hire a 4x4, preferably with a knowledge-able driver. A day trip into the mountains will reveal ancient rock art, mountain villages that are still only reachable by donkey, lock houses in situ and breath-taking views into the fjords and along the east coast. The view of the beautiful **Khawr Najd** fjord (about 24km/15 miles southeast of Khasab) is particularly memorable – from the vantage point a series of hairpin bends lead down to the sea.

The road from Khasab climbs steeply up to the

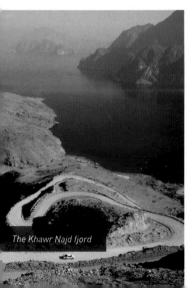
The Khawr Najd fjord

Sayh Plateau. A rare flat piece of land in the otherwise convoluted landscape, it is cultivated with wheat and onions. Across the plateau, the road climbs further towards Jabal Harim (2,087 metres/6,847ft), the highest point in Musandam. The highest drivable point is at 1,687 metres (5,534ft), directly below the radar station which marks the summit, from where the views

### Bait al Qufi

These unique stone buildings, or 'lock houses', which are half built underground, have been used as granaries for hundreds of years. Stores of seasonal produce grown in the mountains are locked up for safety when families move down to the coast in the summer months to supplement their diet by catching fish.

are stunning. Just a short walk from the car park are some ancient petroglyphs showing human figures and animals.

The road descends abruptly, affording views of cavernous wadis, and leads to the coastal town of **Daba**, the southern entry point into Musandam. Still often referred to as Dibba, it is split into three areas of control under Oman, and the emirates of Sharjah and Fujairah. Towards the northern end of the long bay is the Atana Khasab Hotel, and two bays further north is Zighy Bay and its famous Six Senses Luxury Resort.

Midway between the Musandam peninsula and Oman proper, the Omani town of **Madha** ⑲ is a real oddity. The villagers of this tiny, well-watered enclave elected to join Oman when the peninsula was divided amongst the new entities emerging in the 1960s. Totally surrounded by the emirates of Fujairah, Ras al Khaimah and Sharjah, the main point of interest is a small private museum presenting Madha's unique history. Amazingly, there is an even smaller enclave completely within Madha called Nahwa, which belongs to Sharjah.

Snorkelling at the Khawr Sham fjord in Musandam

# WHAT TO DO

Oman offers plenty of activities for young and old, with as much adventure as you can handle. There are some amazing off-road 4x4 drives in the mountains and gorges, and great opportunities for trekking through the mountain wilderness or more gentle hikes along the wadis. Watersport enthusiasts will revel in Oman's enormous coastline, which also offers naturalists some exceptional bird-watching, not to mention the many dive centres which have opened up an amazing, pristine underwater world. Shoppers can bargain for gold, frankincense and myrrh at the colourful souqs and bargain-hunt in bustling malls. At the end of the day there's no shortage of nightlife, with bars, clubs and live music.

## SPORTS AND OUTDOOR ACTIVITIES

Oman is trying hard to position itself on the international sporting map, but faces stiff competition from its neighbours attempting the same thing. In 2009 Oman hosted the Football Gulf Cup of Nations, which it won for the first time in its history, defeating Saudi Arabia in the final. In 2010 it played host to the Asian Beach Games, centred on the coastal town of Al Musanaah and saw the first running of the Tour of Oman professional six-day cycling race which continues annually. In 2012 it hosted the Beach Handball World Championship and in 2014 the final event of the RC44 Championship Tour ended in Muscat. For the first time in 2016 Formula One came to Oman for a Red Bull F1 Showrun. Oman will continue to attract more international events in the upcoming years.

**Scuba-diving.** Most beach hotels have a dive centre, a number of which are run by the Extra Divers organisation, www.

*Experience the raw beauty of the desert and mountains in a 4x4*

extradivers.info. These include Salalah, Mirbat, Al Sawadi, Khasab, Zighy Bay and Muscat's established operation at the Oman Dive Centre (Quantab Beach), which has developed from a few beach cabins in the mid-1990s into a major dive centre with all facilities, including a beachside restaurant. Further along the coast is the Shangri-La Barr al Jissah Resort, with its own dive centre. Most dive boats offer spare places for snorkellers if conditions are suitable.

**Desert safaris and off-road driving.** The mountains and desert interior of Oman are perfect places for 4x4 adventures. Popular day and weekend excursions give a real taste of the rugged environment, and there are few restrictions on where to go. Nowadays the use of powerful 4x4 vehicles makes this possible for everyone, but there are still risks involved, and every off-road journey should be well equipped and organised. The most popular 4x4 routes are dramatic traverses through the gorges of the Jabal al Akhdar Mountains, such as Wadi Bani Awf, which links Rustaq with Nizwa. The track gets very steep in places and gives access to Snake Canyon for some optional canyoning adventures. Routes and details are available from various publications. Visitors can arrange desert expeditions themselves, planning to camp overnight, but local knowledge is invaluable, and there should always be an experienced person responsible for navigation, communication, equipment and emergency procedures. Never go into the mountains or desert with just a single vehicle. Local tour operators organise desert tours (see page 122).

**Walking and trekking.** Popular and easy wadi walks include Wadi Shab and Wadi Tawi on the coastal side of the Eastern Hajar Mountains, and Wadi Bani Khalid on the inland side. Even the most gentle trek should be well prepared and equipped. Invest in a good map and always take plenty of water. Many tour companies offer organised walks and treks of varying degrees of difficulty, which are a safer option for the less experienced hiker.

**Sailing.** Windy conditions for most of the year make sailing a popular pastime. For details of tuition, events and races, contact the Ras al Hamra Sailing Club (tel: +968 2467 8759; www. rahsc.weebly.com), which has Hobie Cats and Laser dinghies, as well as Optimists and Toppers for younger members. The Club also offers diving, fishing, kayaking and powerboating.

## ⊙ DIVE SITES OF OMAN

South of Muscat, the popular dive sites at Bandar Khayran boast over 200 species of fish, 40 types of coral and the wreck of the *Al Munassir*, an 84-metre (275ft) naval ship sunk as an artificial reef. The whole Bandar Khayran area is set for further development as a diving and snorkelling centre. Find more about diving in this area at www.euro-divers.com. The Daymaniyat Archipelago, 18km (11 miles) off Barka on the Batinah coast, is a protected nature reserve of nine islands, with 20 dive locations easily accessible from the Al Sawadi Beach Resort, www.extradivers. info. More remote dive sites off Salalah, Mirbat and Musandam are almost pristine, but more suited to experienced divers.

Sailboats, kayaks and canoes are available at the Al Bustan Palace Hotel and other beach resorts.

**Watersports.** The long coastline offers excellent opportunities for watersports from windsurfing, kitesurfing and wakeboarding to water-skiing and jet-skiing. With almost constant winds, kitesurfing is extremely popular. At Az Zaibah Beach, near Muscat, a six-hour beginner course is run by Kitesurfing Lessons (tel: +968 9400 6007; www.kitesurfing-lessons.com). Jet skis can be hired by the hour at the As Sawadi Beach Resort.

**Sport fishing.** Most large tour operators can organise deep-sea fishing excursions (see page 122), but there are several specialists, including Sidab Sea Tours (tel: +968 9946 1834; www.sidabseatours.com), which also offer dolphin-watching and snorkelling trips. Or try the fishing section of the Ras al Hamra Boat Club (www.fishing.pdorc.com). Some hotels also offer game fishing. Commonly caught fish include yellow-fin tuna, sailfish and barracuda.

**Dhow cruises.** Sidab Sea Tours (tel: +968 9946 1834; www.sidabseatours.com), and Alsansool Sea Tours (tel: +968 9274 8669; www.alsansool.net), both operate dhow cruises from Mutrah harbour, as well as snorkelling and dolphin-watching trips.

**Semi-submersible.** The *Al Khayran* (tel: +968 2473 7286; www.marinaoman.net/about.php is a semi-submersible craft that takes up to 28 passengers on an 'underwater tour' to observe the coral reefs and marine life. Tours leave Marina Bandar al Rowdha daily at 8, 9, 10 and 11am and transfer to Bandar Khayran, where the semi-sub is stationed.

**Swimming and public beaches.** Many resort hotels, such as the Al Bustan Palace and Crowne Plaza Muscat, have long stretches of white sandy beach within safe lagoons or sheltered bays that are ideal for swimming. But there are also good public beaches in the centre of many major towns such as Sur, Sohar

Sanaw camel market

and Khasab, with picnic spots, shade awnings, showers and toilet facilities. Note that for safety reasons swimming is not permitted along the Salalah beaches during summer months due to the rough *khareef* weather. In accordance with Islamic tradition, all beach visitors should be modestly dressed.

**Horse- and camel-riding.** The most central horse-riding school in Muscat is the Qurm Equestrian Riding School, next to Qurm Natural Park (tel: +968 9983 2199; www.qe.hashimani. com; daily 8.30–11am and 4–8pm). It has over 40 horses for both novice and experienced riders, and a 90-minute ride includes access to the beach. Their centre at Barka offers more extensive half-day horse treks. Horse and camel rides along the beach and coastal plains depart from the Al Sawadi Beach Resort (tel: +968 2679 5545).

**Bird-watching.** Spring (Mar–May) and Autumn (Aug–Nov) are good times to observe birds migrating between wintering in

Africa and summer breeding in Asia. The water pools of the wadis attract herons and kingfishers, and are important resting points for birds flying across Arabia. For listings and more information, visit the Ornithological Society of the Middle East website (www.osme.org).

**Golf.** Golfing facilities in Oman have vastly improved in recent years. The Muscat Hills Golf and Country Club (tel: +968 2451 4080; www.muscathillsgolf.com), is situated on the hillside opposite Muscat International Airport. Oman's first championship grass golf course has a clubhouse with restaurant and bar. Amateurs as well as professionals can also play at Ghala Valley Golf Club (www. ghalagolf.com) and Almouj Golf (www. almoujgolf.com). The Ras Al Hamra Golf Club offers a nine-hole layout and the first completely floodlit course in Oman. (tel: +968 9910 6039, www.rasalhamragolfclub.com).

**Ten-pin bowling.** Opposite the Ibis and Muscat Holiday hotels at Al Khuwayr is Oman Bowling Centre (tel: +968 2448 0747; Sat–Wed 8.30pm–2am; Thu, Fri and Sun 10am–2am), with 10 lanes. Al Masa Bowling (tel: +968 2469 3991), inside the Al Masa Mall at Al Shati, has 16 lanes.

### Ali al Habsi

The most famous Omani sportsman is football goalkeeper Ali al Habsi, who has represented Oman since 2002. He became the first Omani player in the English Premier League when he signed for Bolton Wanderers in 2006. Later he played for Wigan Athletic.

## SPECTATOR SPORTS

**Football.** The most popular sport in Oman is football, even though the national team has yet to make any great inroads at international level. International matches at the National Stadium in the Sultan Qaboos Sports Complex at Bawshar are well attended.

Barefoot football

**Camel- and horse-racing.** Races are usually held on Friday and national holiday mornings during the winter months, but getting advance information can be difficult. The daily newspaper websites sometimes make last-minute announcements. Betting is not permitted.

# ENTERTAINMENT

Several venues including the Royal Opera House host concerts and theatrical performances. Most of the regular nightlife though revolves around bars and nightclubs within the larger hotels, especially at weekends. Some places strictly enforce dress codes, so keep it smart casual. Check listings at hotels, on websites or in local magazines.

**Bars and nightclubs.** Popular bars in Muscat hotels include the Lounge at the Al Falaj and Club Safari and Habana Sports

Bar at the Grand Hyatt(see page 136). Overlooking Qurm Natural Park is the trendy Left Bank lounge bar (tel: +968 2469 3699, www.thebank.co) with terrace and indoor seating, serving cocktails and an à la carte menu. One of the top nightclubs in Muscat is the Copacabana at the Grand Hyatt (tel: +968 2464 1234; Mon–Fri 10pm–2am, open until 3am on Thursdays), whose nautically themed John Barry Bar is highly rated. Some bars attract a loyal clientele for their live television sports coverage, especially the English premier leagues in football and rugby, including Duke's Bar at the Crowne Plaza (tel: +968 2457 4442) and Churchill's at the Muscat Holiday Hotel (tel: +968 2439 9100). The Sama Terrazza rooftop lounge at the Park Inn (tel: +968 2450 7888) is a great place to unwind with a drink and laidback music. Outside of the major hotels, alcohol is not available at many restaurants.

**Live music.** The Royal Opera House (tel: +968 2440 3300; www.rohmuscat.org.om) hosts, besides opera, a variety of classical and jazz concerts as well as ballet performances. Many hotel bars have live music at least one night a week, mostly rock and pop. The Majan Continental has a live music venue – the Arab-themed Oasis Bedouin show. The Pub on the eighth floor of the Al Falaj

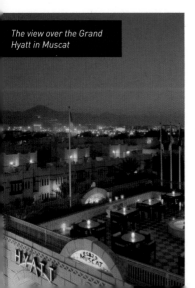

*The view over the Grand Hyatt in Muscat*

has great views and a lively atmosphere. In Salalah there is live music nightly at Whispers Lounge in the Hilton.

**Cinemas.** Hollywood and Bollywood blockbusters are likely to be playing at the cinemas in Oman. City Cinema (CC) has multiple-screen theatres at Al Shati, Ruwi, Sohar, Sur, Muscat Grand Mall, Buraimi, Salalah. Schedules and online booking at citycinemaoman.net . Also check www.albahjacinema.net.

**Art galleries.** For contemporary art and photography, check out the Bait Muzna Gallery in Old Muscat (see page 29).The Omani Society for Fine Arts (tel: +968 2469 4969), also stages exhibitions and performances. The annual Muscat Art Festival is held in February.

## SHOPPING

Oman has many opportunities for great-value shopping at its various modern malls (generally Sat–Thu 10am–10pm) and its more traditional souqs such as Mutrah (9am–1pm and 4–9pm, closed Friday morning). Beyond the airport is City Centre Muscat (tel: +968 2455 8888; www.citycentremuscat.com; Sat–Thu 10am–10pm, Fri 2–10pm), with 150 stores, including a Carrefour hypermarket (9am–midnight) and more than 20 eateries. The smaller Qurm City Centre (tel: +968 2447 0700; www.qurumcitycentre.com; daily 10am–10pm) also has a Carrefour hypermarket (9am–midnight) and 75 outlets. Next to the Royal Opera House the chic Opera Galleria (tel: +968 2494 6100; daily 10am–10pm) has elegant boutiques and designer stores. Try independent shops for more unusual souvenirs, such as wedding jewellery, metal coffee pots and traditional Omani *khanjar* daggers.

**Gold and silver.** Mutrah Souq (see page 34) is the obvious choice, where gold is sold according to its price that day, with a consideration for the workmanship involved. Salalah has a gold and silver souq just south of the Sultan Qaboos Mosque. Large gold retailers include Gallery Argan, and Damas, www. damasjewel.com, both with several outlets around Muscat.

**Perfume.** As well as taking back some frankincense and myrrh, a unique gift from Oman would be the locally produced Amouage perfume, based on ancient aromatics. There are several outlets, including one in the departure lounge at Muscat Airport, but a visit to the Amouage Perfumery at the start of the Nizwa highway is great for sampling the choices (see page 40).

**Artwork.** For high-quality gifts, look around Bait Muzna Gallery (tel: +968 2460 7006; www.baitmuznagallery.com; Sat–Thu 9.30am–7pm), which offers Oman-inspired original artwork and limited-edition prints by leading contemporary and international artists. It also stocks a fine range of hand-screened textiles, soft cotton-blend scarves, stoneware pottery, framed photographs, jewellery and cards. Another good source of arty items is Al Madina Art Gallery (tel: +968 2469 1380, www. almadinaartgallery.com) at 145/6 Al Inshirah Street, Madinat As Sultan Qaboos.

### Bargaining

Even if you don't like haggling over prices, it is all part of the buying process in smaller independent shops, especially for jewellery, carpets and souvenirs. As a rule, try to settle for about half the initial price, or get something extra for free. Prices in shopping malls are fixed.

**Books and publications.** Some hotel bookshops sell informative tourist books on Oman, but there are few specialist shops for detailed publications of the region. The two branches of WHSmith at Muscat International Airport have a good selection at arrivals and departures. The House of Prose Bookshop (tel: +968 9380 3435) at Al Wadi Centre has a vast

*Shopping for carpets at Mutrah Souq*

selection of books in a wide range of categories. The Oman Children Bookstore in Muscat will customise their books for children using a unique story line and them as the central character.

**Local art, craft and antiques.** In Muscat, visit the Omani Heritage Gallery (tel: +968 2469 6974; www.omaniheritage.com; Sat–Thu 10am–8pm), located beside D'Arcy's Kitchen in Jawaharat A'Shati Complex. This non-profit organisation sells an upmarket range of locally produced goods including silver, brass, copper, baskets, weaving, pottery, leather, rugs and jewellery. Just outside the entrance to Nizwa Fort, the Omani Craftsman's House (tel: +968 2451 1451), sells local handicrafts produced by the Sidab Women's Sewing Group, which supports rural communities. If visiting Taqah Fort near Salalah, step inside the Women's Handicrafts Shop for colourful handmade souvenirs such as silver rings, bracelets, clothes and hats as well as incense, perfumes and henna.

# ACTIVITIES FOR CHILDREN

There are several activities aimed at children in the main centres. Horse- and camel-riding, snorkelling cruises, dolphin-watching and sailing are always popular with families.

**Museums.** The Children's Museum in Muscat (see page 36) is an obvious place to take the kids for entertainment and education. There are interactive exhibits to enthral older children and a play area for smaller children. The Oil & Gas Exhibition Centre (see page 36) has lots of hands-on displays and interesting explanations of oil production and conservation, though under-12s need permission to enter. At the same venue, the Planetarium (tel: +968 2467 5542; www.pdo.co.om/pages/planetarium.aspx; booking essential; free) has shows in English every Wednesday, plus there's a programme of live stargazing events. The Natural History Museum (see page 38) has some fossil quizzes aimed at children as well as plenty of stuffed animals, and of course the ever-popular suspended whale skeleton. The Sultan's Armed Forces Museum (see page 35) has an outdoor area of tanks, planes, rockets and missiles.

**Paintball.** As popular with the grown-ups as it is with

*Oman is a very child-friendly, family-oriented country*

*A colourful variety of reef fish can be seen at the Aquarium*

the kids, Paintball Oman (tel: +968 9850 0777; www.paintball oman.com) has a 5,000-sq-metre (54,000-sq-ft) grass field on the road to Sohar/Seeb.

**Ice-skating.** Ice-skating is the complete antidote to life in the hot city, and Muscat's Ice-Skating Centre (see page 38) remains as popular as ever since it first opened in the 1990s. There is another larger ice rink in the Fun Zone (tel: +968 2466 2951; www.funzoneoman.com; Sat–Fri 9am–midnight), next to Al Qurm Park, which also features a bowling alley and a gaming centre. Mondays are ladies only.

**Horse-riding.** See Qurm Equestrian Riding School (see page 87).

**Public parks.** Every town and city has shaded public parks, with slides, swings and climbing frames for younger children, which usually open at 4pm, being extremely popular in the late afternoon and evening, when the heat abates.

# CALENDAR OF EVENTS

**January–February** The Muscat Festival (www.muscat-festival.com) is a 22-day event celebrating Oman's culture and history with concerts, fashion shows, food festivals, gala dinners, arts events, workshops and lectures accompanied by nightly laser shows and firework displays.

**February–March** The Tour of Oman (www.letour.fr/tour-of-oman) six-stage cycling race, which runs along challenging mountain and coastal roads. Muscat International Book Fair and Muscart Art Festival.

**July–August** Between 15 July and 31 August, the Salalah Tourism Festival celebrates the monsoon season, when the southernmost tip of Oman transforms from a dry desert to a lush green carpet. It attracts up to 2 million visitors with music, dancing and parades. A visit to Mughsayl is popular, as the rough seas create large blow holes of exploding sea water.

**November** National Day celebrations on and around the birthday of HM Sultan Qaboos on 18 November.

**November–December** Bank Muscat Shopping Festival. Shops try to outdo each other with attractive prices, extended opening hours, entertainment, prize draws and free offers.

**November–March** Camel-racing at various racetracks around the country.

### Festivals fixed by Islamic calendar

*Al Hijra* Islamic New Year
*12 Rabiul Awal* Birthday of Prophet Muhammad
*Lailat al Miraj* Prophet Muhammad's Ascension
*1 Ramadan* Start of the month of Ramadan
*Eid al Fitr* Celebrates the end of Ramadan for up to five days
*Eid al Adha* Commemorates the sacrifice of Abraham (up to nine days)
Check exact dates with tour operators and websites, as they change year by year.

 **EATING OUT**

Oman offers a wide variety of local and international cuisines to meet the demands of the many nationalities living and working here. Menus are a delicious combination of Persian, Middle Eastern, Indian and Far Eastern influences, with some East African flavours thrown into the mix. For thousands of years the *falaj* water system has channelled water from natural springs to irrigate large areas of fertile land, much of it being silt washed down from the mountains. Dates are the main crop of the Batinah plain, but limes, mangoes, bananas and other fruits are also grown, as well as tomatoes, onions and aubergines. The cultivated fields also provide fodder and grazing for

*A wide variety of produce is grown on the fertile Batinah plain*

livestock and poultry, hence the availability of fresh meat, a rarity in Arabia until recent times. Oman's position along the Gulf of Oman and extensive Indian Ocean coastline also assure a plentiful supply of fresh fish and seafood.

## WHERE TO EAT

For the best international food from Iran, Europe, China and Japan, head for the specialist restaurants in the hotels. The best Indian and Pakistani food is usually found at smaller restaurants catering for the army of workers from South Asia employed in the main towns of the Sultanate. For the most part African, Egyptian and Omani food is best sampled in local

### ⦿ RAMADAN

The Islamic month of fasting, Ramadan throws working hours and mealtimes into disarray, especially outside of the hotels. The vast majority of the population are Muslim and do not eat, drink or smoke during the hours of daylight, but non-Muslims are permitted discreetly to use the restaurants and cafés that remain open within the hotels. Non-Muslims cannot eat, drink or smoke outdoors in public, and the sale of alcohol is severely restricted, even inside some hotels. Immediately after sunset everyone breaks the fast by eating the *iftar* meal. Drinking (water and soft drinks only) and having fun can carry on right through the night. The early-morning meal is the final one before daylight. Additional social events are sometimes organised purely for Ramadan, and it can be an opportunity to sample local food, not otherwise available. Keep an eye out for communal meals offered at cultural, social or sporting centres as part of their special Ramadan activities.

eating places, often without a name, which prepare
dishes enjoyed by the local
population. Vegetarians
are well catered for, with
many South Indian and
vegetarian restaurants,
mostly in the main centres.

For consistent quality
and service, the largest
hotels are the most reli-
able, with prices to match.
They employ top chefs
who prepare a wide range
of international dishes.
Independent restaurants

Al Bustan hotel chef

run by expats from many nations offer very reasonably priced
menus and are great places to sample a vast range of dishes
and culinary styles. Some of these smaller independent establishments are now allowed to serve alcohol.

Given the size of Oman, the choice and variety on offer will also
depend largely on where you are. Musandam is very near to Iran,
so its food has many Persian influences. In Dhofar, which has
links with Africa, you can sample some unforgettable speciali-
ties such as hot bread wrapped around cheese and honey. Most
ingredients are fresh and sourced from local farms and gardens.

## WHEN TO EAT

Breakfast timings in the hotels are quite extensive, roughly
between 6.30am and 11am. Some local restaurants open
early to serve breakfasts to workers, with some cafés having
specialist cuisine from 6am to midday. As most of the offices

Cooking mishkak

and companies shut for the afternoon around 1pm, lunch is generally taken between 1.30pm and 3.30pm and is often the main meal of the day. After lunch, many restaurants close until the evening. Evening meals tend to be taken between 8pm and 10pm, and reservations might be necessary on Thursday and Friday evenings at popular restaurants. Hotels are mindful that Westerners and many tourists prefer to eat earlier, and serve food accordingly. Many clubs and hotels offer Friday deals on inclusive food, buffets or barbecues, which are extremely popular with families at weekends. Most restaurants are very tolerant of children, but few provide special seating or child-friendly menus, so if these are needed it is best to enquire in advance.

## WHAT TO EAT

For most visitors, breakfast will be a large buffet laid on by the hotel, usually with a huge choice of breads, pastries, salads, fruit, cold meats and hot dishes made to order by a chef. Often there will be a typical Arab dish, such as *fuul*, made from broad fava beans, ladled out from a large, steaming metal pot. *Fuul* comes in a wide variety of styles and is a popular and filling dish to start the day. *Fuul Medammes* is seasoned with cumin, olive oil, lemon and spices, but there are always plenty of accompaniments to add, such as tomatoes, onions and peppers. A more unusual local Arabian breakfast is *lokhemat* – deep-fried flour and yeast dumplings infused with cardamom and served with sweet lime or date syrup (not for the calorie-conscious!). Many places open early for European-style breakfasts, including several branches of Kargeen Caffe in the central malls.

The internationalisation of Oman in general, and the Greater Muscat area in particular, means that you have a choice of cuisines from around the world. Western-style cafés are

## ◉ OMANI FOOD

A traditional Omani meal depends on your location. Near to the coast, the locals catch plenty of fish and seafood, and have a great tradition of grilling, frying and baking fish, usually with rice. Towards Dhofar, a fried fish and rice dish is known as *Ruz al Mudhroub*. A time-honoured way of using surplus fish is to dry it, and you can still sometimes see salted dried fish on sale at inland souqs. In the mountains, lamb is eaten in various forms, such as *mishkak* – kebabs grilled on open charcoal fires. In the environs of the desert, the staple diet is dates, milk and occasionally camel meat. It would have to be a very special occasion indeed, as camels are far too valuable to be killed just for their meat, as they provide transport, milk and wealth for the entire family.

Falafel makes for a cheap and tasty snack

widespread, offering great varieties of coffee and comfort food like muffins, pastries and cookies. Outside in the back-streets, especially in Ruwi, Bawshar and Al Khuwayr, are little neighbourhoods that could easily be in Cairo, Beirut, Baghdad or Mumbai, all selling their own types of bread and food to devoted clients. A number of outlets under the name 'Automatic Restaurant' serve wonderful Lebanese dishes quickly and at great value. Other franchises serve great Indian food at restaurants like Saravanaa Bhavan (South Indian vegetarian) and Copper Chimney (Mumbai), both of which are recommended.

The Arabic convenience foods such as *shawarmas* (giant skewers of meat, often lamb, cooked on a vertical spit, then sliced, topped with *tahina* or yoghurt and salad served in pitta bread), and falafel (deep-fried chickpea balls) make cheap and tasty snacks on the move.

Menus for lunch and dinner tend to be quite similar, starting with a few plates of appetisers or *mezze*, which in themselves can be quite substantial. Originally cuisine from the Levant and in particular Lebanon, these dishes have established themselves as universal Arabian food and are very popular around the Middle East. Classic dishes include *hummus*, an international staple made from chickpeas, garlic and oil; *tahina*, a thin paste made from ground sesame seeds with added olive oil and spices; *babaganugh*, mashed aubergine with garlic, lemon juice and oil; and *moutabbal*, made from roast aubergines and sesame paste. The *mezze* are usually eaten with fresh oven-baked bread.

A popular lunchtime dish is lamb or chicken *makbous*, where the main ingredient is slowly cooked throughout the morning with onions and saffron rice. Seasoned with spices and lime, vegetables of the season are added, such as tomatoes, green peppers or potatoes.

Main dishes for both lunch and dinner include the Indian-inspired *biryani samakh*, 'fish biryani' – rice, spices, vegetables and seafood all cooked together; *laham mashwee*, 'stuffed lamb' – eaten with bread, but also sometimes made from fish. *Kuftah* are meatball kebabs often rolled up in pitta bread with salad and yoghurt. Many places offer main-meal menus with standard dishes such as grilled meats, fish, kebabs and chicken, served with different varieties of rice, as well as pasta dishes, soups and salads.

An invitation should always be accepted to a wedding or special seasonal celebration, when you might partake of traditional dishes served on a large platter, around which the guests sit on the floor. When instructed by your hosts, just dig in, but make sure to use only the right hand. One such opportunity is at the end of the fasting month of Ramadan, celebrated by *Eid al Fitr*, when everyone is in a joyous mood. One of the

In coastal areas, fish is the staple diet

favourite meals is *harees*, a kind of porridge made from pieces of meat (usually lamb) and whole wheat. The wheat is cooked in a pot, to which the meat is added and left for another few hours. This mixture is then transferred to an oven (or buried under hot coals if in the desert) and cooked for a few more hours until ready to serve.

*Shuwa* is the traditional celebratory village meal in Oman when a whole animal (cow, goat, lamb or sometimes a young camel) is roasted in an underground pit for up to two days, until the meat is tender enough to drop from the bone. Herbs, spices and pepper might be added to create a unique flavour. It is usually served on giant platters as chunks of meat lying on a bed of rice and other ingredients, into which everyone digs with their right hands.

True Omani food is hard to find outside the home. The best place to sample authentic Omani dishes is at the more stylish Omani restaurants such as Ubhar (see page 110), where you can sample a delicious shuwa, and Kargeen Caffe (see page 108), both in Muscat.

## DESSERTS

**Arabic coffee**

Local Arabic coffee, known as *qahwa*, is taken thick and strong, often with dates or something sweet like *halwa* to complement the strong and bitter taste.

*Halwa* is a generic name for dessert or sweetmeats, but it also refers to a special Omani dessert made from eggs, sugar, ghee, nuts, cornflower, rosewater and cardamom. A large number of patisseries and cake shops are spread across Muscat, and many of the sweet, sticky pastries will be familiar from Greece, Turkey or Lebanon. *Baklava* is a light filo pastry stuffed with honey and pistachio nuts. *Kunafa* is similar but made with a more delicate shredded pastry. *Basboosa* is a semolina cake, dripping with syrup and lemon. Omani dates often feature, either as an ingredient in cakes, puddings, rolls or pastry, or more exotically in date ice cream.

## DRINKS

Alcohol is served in most major hotels and clubs whose restaurants, bars and nightclubs are often lively establishments, especially at weekends. Coffee shops and cafés are located all over Muscat, serving a wide choice of coffees, snacks and pastries. Locals drink *laban*, salty buttermilk, and yoghurt drinks flavoured with spices and nuts, while date juice is a local speciality.

The communal smoking of a *shisha* (*nargile* or hubble-bubble) water pipe is something that you will see in many pavement and rooftop cafés. The thick, pungent tobacco is usually mixed with other flavours such as molasses or apple. This

activity is not confined to old men. It is quite common to see groups of young people of both sexes sharing a *shisha* in one of the open-air beachside restaurants.

## TO HELP YOU ORDER...

**I am a vegetarian** ana nabatee (male)/ana nabateeya (female)

**Please** men fadlak

**thank you** shukran

**the bill, please** fattoura, men fadlak

## MENU READER

**ananas** pineapple
**aruz** rice
**baith** eggs
**baleyan** aubergine
**basal** onions
**batata** potato
**beera** beer
**bidun laham** without meat
**burtogal** oranges
**dajaj** chicken
**filfil** pepper
**fuul** beans
**gambari/rubian** prawns/ shrimps
**haleeb** milk
**hummus** chickpeas
**jeh** watermelon
**jibna** cheese
**khall** vinegar

**khubz** bread
**kibdah** liver
**kuftah** meatballs
**lahm** meat
**makaruna** pasta
**maya** water
**milh** salt
**nabeeth** wine
**qahwa** coffee
**salata** salad
**samakh** fish
**samn** butter
**shai** tea
**shakkar** sugar
**shokalata** chocolate
**shorbah** soup
**tamat** tomatoes
**toofa** apple
**zaytoun** olives

# PLACES TO EAT

Expect to pay the following for a three-course meal for one person:

| | |
|---|---|
| $$$$ | over 25 RO |
| $$$ | 12–25 RO |
| $$ | 6–12 RO |
| $ | below 6 RO |

## MUSCAT

**Al Boom $$** *Marina Hotel, opposite the fish market, Mutrah Corniche, tel: +968 2471 3100.* Great views over Mutrah and the harbour from the top-floor terrace of this hotel restaurant, but the balcony is narrow, so outside seating is limited. Good honest Mediterranean and Middle Eastern food, also serving alcohol.

**Al Khiran Terrace $$$–$$$$** *Al Bustan Palace Hotel, south of Old Muscat, tel: +968 2479 9666.* Buffet-style dining throughout the day. Themed cuisines from Europe to the Far East and à la carte choices accompanied by fine wines. Indoor and outdoor dining, overlooking the pristine beach. Very popular.

**Al Angham $$$–$$$$** *Royal Opera House, tel: +968 2207 7777*, www.alanghamoman.com. This top-end, award winning restaurant offers Omani décor and specialities including *shiwa*, *harees*, *jareesh* and *o'rsyia*. A meal in this restaurant could be the perfect start or end to a night at the opera. Freshly squeezed juices and fruit cocktails make up for the fact that the restaurant does not have an alcohol licence. For dessert, try the delicious frankincense ice cream.

**Automatic Restaurant $** *Qurm, tel: +968 2448 7200; Al Khuwayr, tel: +968 2448 7200; Al Ghubrah, tel: +968 2449 9981; Seeb, tel: +968 9265 4739.* Many outlets for this ever-popular chain, serving good-value Lebanese and Middle Eastern food. No alcohol.

**Beach Restaurant $$$–$$$$** *Chedi Hotel, North Ghurba 32, Way No. 3215 18th November Street, tel: +968 2452 4343*. Superb Far Eastern and European seafood served in a luxurious private beach setting, overlooking the Gulf of Oman. Exclusive and expensive, but ideal for that special meal or memorable occasion. Seafood dishes with an international twist, such as mussels with kaffir lime and coconut or lobster tail carpaccio. Grilled fish is another local delicacy. Open for dinner only Sept–May. No shorts allowed.

**Copper Chimney $** *Fairtrade House, Mutrah Business District, Ruwi, tel: +968 2470 6420*. Franchise of the original Mumbai restaurant, providing excellent North Indian food in the middle of the business district. Watch your food being cooked through the windows into the kitchen. No alcohol.

**D'Arcy's Kitchen $–$$** *Jawaharat a'Shati Complex, tel: +968 2469 9119*, www.darcyskitchen.letseat.at. Friendly, efficient European-style pavement café serving reasonably priced Western food in a pleasant atmosphere. Popular with both expats and visitors. Open daily, 8.30am–10.30pm. Next to the Omani Heritage Gallery.

**Fisherman's Lodge $$$** *Way 2241, Qurm, tel: +968 2456 8790*. Fine seafood dining for a dedicated clientele in a tiny restaurant also operating as a fish supplier. Egyptian chef Tarek has 35 years' experience preparing fish in top hotels. Not easy to find, but worth it for the fabulous dishes. From the roundabout near Japengo Café, head inland towards the Qurm Natural Park entrance along Al Qurm Street. At the top of a small hill, turn left into Way 2241. Open 11.30am–4.30pm and 6.30–11pm. No alcohol.

**Japengo Café $$–$$$** *Al Shati Street, tel: +968 9289 2868*. Stunning location for this uber-cool beachside location with UAE origins. Serves traditional Western food, often with an Eastern twist, as well as oriental, Chinese and Japanese sushi dishes. Good wood-fired pizzas. Great place to hang out, especially the upstairs shisha terrace. No alcohol.

**Kargeen Caffe $–$$** *Madinat as Sultan Qaboos, tel: +968 2469 9055*, www.kargeen.com. There are now several branches of the Kargeen Caffe around Muscat, but this delightfully laidback 'oasis café' is the original.

Sit on cushioned benches under shady trees and choose from a wide range of traditional Omani grills, or Middle Eastern or Western dishes, accompanied by specialist teas, coffees and mocktails (without alcohol).

**La Brasserie $$–$$$** *opposite fish market, Mutrah Corniche, tel: +968 9137 1999.* A bistro where fish prepared by a French chef is the speciality. Spread over three floors, with stunning views across the harbour from the third-floor terrace. Top-quality French cuisine. No alcohol.

**Left Bank $$–$$$** *below Mumtaz Mahal Restaurant, Qurm, tel: +968 2469 3699,* www.thebank.co. Lounge-bar dining at its best. Make a reservation for the terrace to watch the sun set over Qurm Natural Park. Very popular for homemade Sunday lunch and Friday Sundowner menu. Extensive wine list and cocktails.

**Miabin $$** *Majan Continental, Al Ghubrah Street, tel: +968 2459 2900.* 24-hour coffee shop and international dining restaurant. Excellent à la carte Indian food for lunch or dinner. Themed evening buffets, with Monday's Indian and Wednesday's Tandoori the best choices.

**Mumtaz Mahal Restaurant $$–$$$** *Qurm, tel: +968 2460 5907.* Distinctive white hilltop building overlooking Qurm Natural Park, just after the Royal Opera House along the main highway. Continually maintains its high quality to justify being the most expensive of all the Indian restaurants in Muscat.

**Sama Terrazza $$$** *Park Inn, Al Khuwayr, tel: +968 2450 7888.* This seventh-floor rooftop lounge is fabulously colourful, with pool, bar, great views and sometimes live music at weekends. Comfortable sofa seats for lounging and drinking or tables for eating. Their 'Seafood Grill @ Sundown' is a popular eat-all-you-can attraction on a Tuesday evening. Open Sept–Apr daily 6pm–1am.

**Saravanaa Bhavan $** *Hormuz Building, near Ruwi roundabout, tel: +968 2470 4502,* www.saravanabhavan.com. Franchise of award-winning Tamil Nadu vegetarian restaurants. A varied menu with excellent thali, dosa and biryani. Look no further for the best South Indian food in Muscat. No alcohol.

**Shang Thai** $$ *Muscat Grand Mall, 1st floor, Tilal Al Khuwayr, tel: +968 2200 6644*. Tasty Thai food in a modern setting. Extensive menu with vegetarian and non-vegetarian options. The seafood dishes are particularly good. Also available for delivery.

**Shiraz** $$$–$$$$ *Crowne Plaza Hotel, Qurm, tel: +968 2466 0660*. Authentic Persian cuisine served in an intimate atmosphere with a choice of indoor or terrace dining. Barbecue- and seafood-themed nights. Open for lunch and dinner, with stunning views along the coast at night.

**Ubhar** $$–$$$ *Bareeq al Shati Mall, tel: +968 2469 9826*, www.ubhar oman.com. Top-quality Omani food specialising in a variety of meat dishes. If available, try shuwa – beef slowly cooked for 24 hours – the camel biryani or lamb fattah. Open daily 12.30–3.30pm and 6.30–11pm. Reservations essential for Thursday and Friday. No alcohol. Just east of the new Royal Opera House.

## NIZWA

**Bahjat al Sham** $$ *Al Diyar Hotel, Nizwa, tel: +968 2541 2402*, www.aldiyar hotel.com. Good choice of Lebanese, Arabian and Indian food, especially the mezze and grills. Generous portions. Out of Nizwa centre on the way to Muscat.

**Peppercorns Restaurant** $$–$$$ *Nizwa, tel: +968 9963 3811*. Serves mainly Indian dishes but also offer some selections of Chinese and continental meals. Good food and friendly staff. Located at Firq Square.

## SOHAR AND BATINAH COAST

**Africa Coffee House and Restaurant** $–$$ *Butterfly Hotel Suites, Sohar, tel: +968 2684 3501*. Good choice of fresh seafood and meat dishes with an interesting and unusual African menu featuring such specialities as *ndizi* (cooked green bananas) and *mhogo* (cassava in coconut sauce). Part of the new building next door to the Sohar Beach Resort. No alcohol.

**The Restaurant $$$** *Crowne Plaza Hotel, Falaj al Qubail, Sohar, tel: +968 2685 0850*. Elegant hotel restaurant with good à la carte choice of dishes from Italy, North Africa and around the Mediterranean. Delicious desserts. Excellent service. Open for lunch and dinner.

**Mughlai Continental $–$$** *Manam Sohar Hotel Apartments, Sohar, tel: +968 9405 4333*. Arabic, Chinese, Indian and Mandi cuisine. Great-value buffet lunch daily. On the way into Sohar from the Crowne Plaza Hotel.

**Sallan Restaurant and Terrace $$–$$$** *Sohar Beach Hotel, Al Tareef, Sohar, tel: +968 2684 1111, www.soharbeach.com*. Relaxing location for dining through the day, overlooking pool, gardens and sea. Open-air terrace or indoor tables for Arabic, Indian and European cuisine. Dinner served 6–11pm, but light meals are available all day until 3am.

## SUR AND THE EAST

**Oysters Restaurant $$** *Sur Plaza Hotel, Sur, tel: +968 2554 3777*. Wide range of cuisines mainly from the Far East, offered both buffet-style and as à la carte menu. Dishes are prepared using local produce. Open breakfast, lunch and dinner.

**Turtle Reserve $$** *Ras al Jinz, Sur, tel: +968 9655 0606/0707*. Three-course set dinner for up to 40 visitors/diners. Also coffee shop with limited menu available through the day. The food is passable, but this is the only suitable choice for eating in the locality. No alcohol.

## SALALAH AND DHOFAR

**Baalbeck $$** *23rd July Street, Salalah, tel: +968 2329 8834*. In the heart of central Salalah, this traditional Lebanese restaurant offers a great selection of *mezze*, meats and fish. Their family section offers some privacy for those with children. Always popular. No alcohol.

**Darbat Restaurant $$–$$$** *Crowne Plaza Resort, Salalah, tel: +968 2323 8035*. Situated on a terrace overlooking pools and gardens with views down to the beach. The staff are attentive and provide exceptional service. There is a themed buffet dinner every evening. The nearby Dolphin restaurant offers a seafood buffet every night.

**Hassan Bin Thabit $–$$** *23rd July Street, Salalah, tel: +968 2329 1010*, hassanbinthabit.com. This is the most central of several outlets in Salalah offering a varied menu of Indian, Chinese and Western dishes. Don't be put off by the fast-food-style decor – the food is of high quality and very reasonably priced. Near Aqwad roundabout. No alcohol.

**The Island Restaurant $$–$$$** *Juweira Marina, Salalah, tel: +968 9497 2258*. An amazing location that offers incredible sunset views. The menu caters to the expat community with its steaks and burgers. They do offer alcohol.

**Sheba's $$$** *Hilton Resort, Salalah, tel: +968 2321 1234*. The steakhouse offers premium cuts of meat and gorgeous views of the hotel's gardens and the Indian Ocean. Evenings only, 6.30–10.30pm, smart dress required.

# MUSANDAM

**Al Shamaliah Grill $** *Central Square, Khasab, tel: +968 2673 0477*. Best local restaurant in town, serving tasty Omani and Indian dishes to visitors and locals alike. Indoor seating which spills out onto the open central square. Does a roaring takeaway service.

**Al Mawra $$–$$$** *Atana Khasab Hotel, Khasab, tel: +968 2673 0777*. Quality international and Omani food at the best hotel in the area. Specialises in fresh seafood. Spectacular sea views.

**Al Halla Park Restaurant $** *near Al Hallah Park, Al Hallah, Khasab, tel: +968 9922 4777*. Don't be put off by the plastic chairs and tables or the small number of clients as most customers opt for a takeaway. Slightly 'fast food', but still produces good local Omani dishes.

**Poolside Restaurant $$** *Khasab Hotel, Khasab, tel: +968 2673 0267*. Serves a variety of food for visitors during their sightseeing tours around Musandam. Buffet or à la carte seafood choices and popular poolside barbecue. Interior seating if required. Open 7am–11pm.

# A-Z TRAVEL TIPS

## A SUMMARY OF PRACTICAL INFORMATION

## A

## ACCOMMODATION (see also list of Recommended hotels)

The standard and quality of hotels in Oman is high, and so are the prices, but there are some bargains to be had in the off-peak (summer) season or at the newer hotels. During the main tourist season (between October and March) it is wise to reserve your accommodation several weeks in advance. Buying an inclusive flight and hotel package is often better value. Walk-in rates are very expensive, so book online for the best deals, either direct with the hotel or through an online travel agency. There is a shortage of hotels in the lower price range, especially around Muscat. Summer is peak season for the Salalah region because of its cooling *khareef* climate. Credit cards are accepted almost everywhere.

> hotel **fonduq/hotel**
> how much? **bi kum?**

## AIRPORTS

The main arrivals point is **Muscat International Airport**, formerly known as Seeb International Airport (code MCT; flight enquiries tel: +968 2451 9223/9456; www.omanairports.co.om), 30km (18 miles) from the Old Town of Muscat. Passengers who need to obtain a visa on arrival should follow the signs to the Travelex counter. Exchange any currency to buy the visa in Omani Rials (RO). Two receipts are given; one is needed for immigration. After baggage collection there is an X-ray check and duty free for arrivals. Alcohol can be purchased by non-Muslims.

Car hire is available from the airport, or you can take a taxi. The taxi stand is outside the arrivals hall. For reservations contact the Taxi Counter, tel: +968 2434 1297 or email: taxi@omanairports.com.

Fixed rates are displayed in all the major hotels. Journeys into Muscat seldom take more than 40 minutes, except during rush hour. Public buses, run by the Oman National Transport Company, stop on Sultan Qaboos Highway outside of the Muscat International Airport.

At **Salalah Airport** (SLL), there is a list of approved taxi fares on a post outside the terminal, essentially 5 RO within the city, and 7 RO to the more distant hotels. At Khasab (KSB) there are no taxis at the airport and all transfers should be pre-arranged.

## B

## BICYCLE HIRE

Oman's terrain is ideal for off-road mountain biking, and there are some great adventures to be had along the many tracks and trails. Local knowledge is essential for directions and safety. For bike hire and equipment, go to Oman Bicycle (tel: +968 9966 4710; www.oman bicycle.com), located between the Ibis Hotel and Muscat Expressway. For pre-arranged tours, take a look at www.gulfleisure.com/mountain biking.htm. Road cycling is unpopular, as the road network is entirely geared to motor vehicles. Some of the cruise liners rent bikes for easy cycling excursions along Mutrah Corniche.

## BOAT HIRE

Hiring a boat privately can be expensive, so one way to get out to sea is to join one of the commercial dhow tours. A popular excursion is from Mutrah, sailing around the headlands of Old Muscat on a late-afternoon/sunset pleasure cruise. There are daily dhow cruises from Khasab to the Musandam fjords. Most scuba-diving trips can usually accommodate non-divers. Dive boats are a good option for reaching the Daymaniyat Islands. Other boat trips can be organised locally, such as hiring a local boat near the As Sawadi Beach Resort to sail around the offshore islands (for more information and recommended tour operators see page 86 and 122).

## BUDGETING FOR YOUR TRIP

Muscat has good-value flights from some major European airports, but direct flights are more expensive. Hotels can be expensive if not booked in advance or as part of a package. The following prices in RO (Omani Rials) will give you an idea of costs.

**Airport transfer.** Muscat International Airport to city centre 8 RO.

**Car hire.** From 10 RO per day.

**Guides.** Hired through tour agencies from 15 RO for half-day.

**Hotels.** Probably your largest expense, costing 25–250 RO per night.

**Internet cafés.** 0.5–1 RO per hour.

**Meals and drinks.** Breakfasts are normally included in room rates. Set menu or buffet lunch/dinner in four/five-star hotel 10–20 RO. Set menu or buffet lunch/dinner in local restaurant 3–6 RO. Evening meal in downtown restaurant 8–15 RO. Soft drink/coffee in café 1–2 RO.

**Sightseeing.** Admission to forts 0.5–1 RO or attractions 5–10 RO.

**Taxis.** Trip within Old Muscat, Mutrah or Ruwi (up to 5km/3 miles) 3 RO. Within Greater Muscat (including Muscat International Airport) 15 RO.

## C

## CAMPING

Spending the night under the stars amid peaceful sand dunes, on a vast stretch of empty beach or up in the mountains, is a popular pastime for many residents, particularly expats, and visitors. It is permissible to camp almost anywhere, and usually the more remote the better. A few official campsites with toilet and washing facilities do exist around the country, though these are often private concerns (such as for turtle-watching) or are fixed camps on the edge of the desert run by large tour operators (see page 122). Camping tours can be organised by desert-safari operators, with all equipment provided. Those spending a night in the open by themselves should take all equipment with them, including mobile phones and GPS (camping equipment is readily available to buy in Oman) and ensure they leave no rubbish behind.

## CAR HIRE (see also Driving)

Distances between towns can be considerable, and with the lack of public transport, hiring a car is usually a good option. Many companies rent self-drive saloon cars, but if you intend going off-road you must specify a 4x4 vehicle, otherwise you breach rental and insurance agreements. Rental prices and fuel are good value, and it might be cheaper to self-drive than to hire two or three taxis each day. Daily rates start at around 10 RO/day for an economy car, rising to 35 RO/day for a 4x4. The best value is to book and prepay online. Hiring a 4x4 is great for adventure, ideally by those with off-road experience. It's also safer if more than one vehicle takes to the wilds at a time. If you do go it alone, be sure to take all the necessary precautions and be well prepared (plenty of water, extra fuel, a long rope, shovel, spare tyre and jack and base are musts). The cost of hiring a car with a driver for a day, week or month could triple the price, but is less worrisome and worthwhile if you need local knowledge.

To hire a car in Oman you must be at least 25 years of age. An International Driving Permit is better than your national driving licence. Always drive with car-hire documentation and passport for inspection. Major international car-rental companies and some local ones have counters at both Muscat and Salalah airports. Avis has offices at Muscat International Airport (tel: +968 2451 0342; downtown, tel: +968 2440 0888; in Salalah, tel: +968 2320 2581; www.avisoman.com) and inside the largest hotels. Europcar (www.europcar.com) has offices at both Muscat Airport (tel: +968 2452 1369), and Salalah Airport (tel: +968 9943 0608). Thrifty has a 24-hour airport office (tel: +968 2452 1189) and offices at Ruwi, Al Khuwayr, Qurm, Sohar and Salalah. Hertz (www.nttomanhertz.com) is represented by the National Travel and Tourism Agency. There are also several local car-hire companies. Try Mark Rentacar with 24-hour car hire from Muscat International

Airport and downtown locations (tel: +968 2478 6885; www.marktours oman.com/rentacar).

## CLIMATE

Oman has a subtropical climate characterised by hot days, clear, sunny skies and low annual rainfall. The winter months (Oct–Apr) are very pleasant, even if some light rainfall might occur. Winter daytime temperatures reach 25°C (77°F), with cool nights down to 10°C (50°F). During the summer (May–Sept) it can reach 40°C (104°F) and higher, with hot nights. This is the 'off season'. Along the coast there is also high humidity, which can make summer rather uncomfortable. At altitude in the mountains temperatures are much lower, with occasional snow and freezing temperatures in winter. Rainstorms are irregular, but do occur in winter. Dhofar has its own unique climate in summer, when the *khareef* monsoon brings mists and rain from July to September.

|      | J  | F  | M  | A  | M   | J   | J   | A  | S  | O  | N  | D  |
|------|----|----|----|----|-----|-----|-----|----|----|----|----|----|
| °C   | 25 | 26 | 29 | 34 | 39  | 40  | 38  | 36 | 36 | 35 | 30 | 27 |
| °F   | 77 | 79 | 85 | 94 | 103 | 104 | 101 | 97 | 97 | 95 | 86 | 80 |

## CLOTHING

Loose-fitting clothes made from cotton or linen are ideal all year round. Tourists should dress conservatively in towns and cities, covering upper arms and legs. Swimwear is acceptable on private beaches and inside resorts, but err on the conservative side, and topless bathing is not permissible. Bring a sunhat, high-factor sunscreen and sunglasses. In winter always carry a fleece or jacket, as winds can be cold in the desert, at sea or at altitude.

Visitors to the Grand Mosque must wear modest, loose clothing with long sleeves and long skirts or trousers, and women should wear a headscarf. Bring comfortable walking shoes or boots for desert and mountain terrain. Top hotels and resorts have dress codes for their restaurants and bars. Smart casual is the norm for any hotel meal or drink.

## CRIME AND SAFETY

Oman is generally a very safe country, where common sense will avoid potential problems. Beware of pickpockets in crowded places such as bars, hotels and markets. Do not leave valuables unattended when swimming or in cars. If anything is stolen, report it immediately to a police station and obtain a report for insurance purposes (see page 120). The main safety concern is traffic danger. Omanis are not the most cautious of drivers, so when exploring on foot always use pedestrian crossings and be sure to observe the signs.

### D

## DRIVING (see also Car hire)

Driving in Oman is on the right. Traffic jams and parking can be a problem in Ruwi and Mutrah on weekdays. The road system is good, but the general standard of driving is poor, and little courtesy is shown by other drivers, so be on your guard, but avoid offending local cultural norms through abusive gestures or language. Watch out for the bus taxis, which stop or pull out with little notice or indication, and be extra vigilant when driving on roads with tight bends. Some roads in Muscat have average speed cameras which track vehicles over a set distance in order to catch speeding drivers, but away from urban areas, speeds can be frightening, and many cars drive too close. In Dhofar, in particular, be wary of wandering camels. Using a hand-held mobile phone while driving is illegal (headset or Bluetooth is allowed), and seat belts must be worn. If involved in a traffic accident, you must contact the Royal Oman Police immediately (see page 120).

## E

## ELECTRICITY

Electricity supply is good and reliable, using 220v–240v/50Hz current, so most European appliances will be fine, but US goods on 110v require a transformer. Sockets are almost all square three-pin UK standard. Some electrical items are imported and sold with round two-pin plugs, but adaptors are readily available.

## EMBASSIES AND CONSULATES

**Ireland:** Honorary Consulate in Muscat; tel: +968 2470 1282.
**UK:** British Embassy, PO Box 185, Mina al Fahal, Muscat; tel: +968 2460 9000; www.gov.uk/world/organisations/british-embassy-muscat; Sun–Thu 7.30am–2.30pm.
**US:** American Embassy, PO Box 202, Madinat as Sultan Qaboos, Muscat; tel: +968 2464 3400; http://om.usembassy.gov; Sat–Wed 8am–4.30pm.
Oman embassies around the world:
**UK (also responsible for Ireland):** Sultanate of Oman Embassy, 167 Queen's Gate, London, SW7 5HE; tel: 020-7225 0001; www.oman embassy.org.uk; Mon–Fri 9am–3.30pm. Ireland has a Consulate of the Sultanate of Oman, 10a Lower Camden Street, Dublin 2; tel: 01-478 2504; Mon–Fri 9.30am–5.30pm.
**US (also responsible for Canada):** Sultanate of Oman Embassy, 2535 Belmont Road, NW, Washington DC, 20008; tel: 202-387 1980; www.culturaloffice.info; Mon–Fri 9am–4pm. Canada has an Honorary Consulate of the Sultanate of Oman; tel: 514-288 8644; email: omanconsul@bellnet.ca; Mon–Fri 9am–5pm.

Further information can be obtained from the Ministry of Foreign Affairs, www.mofa.gov.om and om.embassyinformation.com.

## EMERGENCIES

In an emergency, call the Royal Oman Police (ROP) on 9999 to alert all the emergency services – police, fire or ambulance. If involved in a road accident, you must not leave the scene or remove vehicles until the police have arrived.

ROP Muscat, tel: +968 2456 0021/2456 2030
ROP Salalah, tel: +968 2329 0099/2329 0103
ROP Nizwa, tel: +968 2542 5099/2542 5559
ROP Sur, tel: +968 2554 0399/2554 2599
ROP Sohar, tel: +968 2684 0099/2684 0096
ROP Buraymi, tel: +968 2565 0199/2565 2998

The ROP website (www.rop.gov.om) is in both Arabic and English, and has useful links, telephone numbers and regional information.

## G

## GAY AND LESBIAN TRAVELLERS

Homosexuality is illegal in Oman, but some couples do have same-sex relationships. Gay and lesbian visitors will encounter few problems as long as they are discreet and cautious about any outward signs of affection towards each other. Local men will often greet each other with kisses and hold hands, but this is not the sign of a gay relationship.

## GETTING THERE (see also Tourist information)

**By air:** Muscat is the hub of the Oman Air network (www.omanair.com), with flights to European, Asian and Middle Eastern cities. Recent expansion and the addition of new runways means the terminal is capable of serving 12 million passengers a year. Major airlines flying directly into Muscat International Airport include British Airways, KLM, Emirates, Etihad, Lufthansa, Swiss International Air Lines and Turkish Airlines. A complete list is available at www.omanairports.com. The other international airport is at Salalah, with links mostly in the Indian subcontinent. In addition, three domestic airports have been built at Sohar, A'Duqm and Ras Al Hadd.

**By road:** The major land border crossing is with Dubai at Hatta, where visitors are usually processed quickly if vehicle and passenger paperwork is correct. The smaller crossing on the coast with Fujairah emirate is at Khitmat Milahah. The border with Abu Dhabi at Buraymi is now fenced, but there are no problems entering from Al Ain. Two entry points are possible for Musandam – the main road from Ras al Khaymah at Tibat or the more remote border post at Dibba (Daba). There are two entry points from Yemen, at Sarfayt on the coast and Al Mazyunah inland.

**By sea:** Muscat is a port of call on most weekly cruises around the Gulf and is often a stop-off on longer worldwide itineraries.

**By rail:** Construction of a 2244km (1519-mile) railway connecting major industrial hubs and cities in Oman is due for completion in 2018. It will form part of the Gulf Railway system designed to connect the members of the Gulf Cooperation Council (GCC): Bahrain, Kuwait, Oman, Qatar, Saudi Arabia, United Arab Emirates and Iraq.

## GUIDES AND TOURS

Some tourist attractions have their own local guides, such as Al Hoota Cave or the Ras al Jinz Turtle Reserve, but you might want to hire your own personal guide to be with you the whole time. Tour agencies can provide vehicle, driver and guide for any number of days, for 4x4 adventures, trekking, riding and camping, or for your own tailor-made itinerary into the mountains or desert.

Some destinations are hard to find without local knowledge. Sightseeing excursions and adventure safaris operated by tour companies are always accompanied by qualified guides. Recommended are:

**Desert Adventures Oman**, P.O. Box 809 Muscat; tel: +968 2469 1300; www.desertadventures.com. Specialize in day and overnight tours.

**Khasab Tours**, PO Box 464, Khasab, Musandam; tel: +968 2673 0464; www.khasabtours.com. Specialists in organising tours and accommodation in Musandam.

**Mark Tours**, PO Box 3310, Al Iskan Street, Ruwi, Muscat; tel: +968 2478 2727; www.marktoursoman.com. Tours, car rental and chauffeur divisions allow full flexibility when organising any tour of Oman.

**NTT Oman Tours**, PO Box 962, Muscat; tel: +968 2466 0300; www.nttomantours.com. Part of the large National Travel & Tourism Company, with many years' experience offering bespoke and group packages and multilingual guides. Many representatives and branches. Agent for Hertz Rent-a-car.

**Zahara Tours**, PO Box 833, Ruwi, Muscat; tel: +968 2440 0844; www.zaharatours.com. Respected large tour operator with over 35 years' experience and a vast fleet of new vehicles, offering many itineraries tailor-made to individual needs and interests.

Several companies specialise in desert safaris and have tented camps on the edge of the Wahibah Sands:

**Desert Discovery Tours**, PO Box 99, Madinat as Sultan Qaboos, Muscat; tel: 968 9200 9427; www.desertdiscovery.com. They offer many itineraries, from half-day to 12-day tours. Owner/operator of Al Naseem Tourism Camp near the Ras al Jinz Turtle Reserve and Al Areesh Desert Camp near Al Qabil. Camps are fenced in and guarded, with accommodation in spacious tents or cabins.

Other desert camps include **Desert Nights** (tel: +968 9281 8388; www.desertnightscamp.com), **Al Raha** (tel: +968 9934 3851; www.alrahaoman.com) and **Nomadic Desert Camp** (+968 9933 6273; www.nomadicdesertcamp.com). **1000 Nights Camp** (tel: +968 9944 8158; www.1000nightscamp.com) offers camping at Wahiba Sands in authentic Bedouin tents equipped toilets and showers, as well as electric charging plugs for those unable to unplug.

## H

# HEALTH AND MEDICAL CARE

The standard of both government and private healthcare in Oman is generally high, with good medical facilities. Apart from some emergency treatment, all medical costs must be paid for, so comprehensive health insurance is highly recommended. Visitors needing hospital treatment will be sent to private hospitals, as government hospitals are reserved for Omani citizens, unless there are no private options. In Muscat the main hospital for tourist emergencies is the United Medical Muscat Private Hospital (Bawshar Street, Al Khuwayr, Muscat; tel: +968 2458 3600; www.muscatprivatehospital.com). The American Specialty Clinics Centre (Al Qurm Street, Way 2235, Building 1693; tel: +968 2456 4200; ascc.om) has American-trained staff and a walk-in service Sat–Thu 9am–9pm.

Stomach upsets are the most common tourist ailment, often due to dehydration, unclean water or change of environment. Excess sun can also cause problems, so always wear a sunhat, sunglasses and use high-factor sunscreen. Drink bottled water and avoid food not freshly cooked.

Bring enough personal medicines with you, but be aware that some regular drugs are restricted (for more information, check www.omanairports.com/customsregulations.asp). For less serious ailments, there are many modern pharmacies for quick, professional advice and medicines. Hotels can always call for an English-speaking doctor or locate an open pharmacy. There is a 24-hour Muscat Pharmacy (www.muscatpharmacy.net) in Ruwi (tel: +968 2470 2542), and in Salalah (tel: +968 2329 1635). A list of duty pharmacies can be found on the Ministry of Health website (www.moh.gov.om).

**Vaccinations:** Nothing compulsory, but recommended for tetanus, typhoid and hepatitis A and B. See www.mdtravelhealth.com for more information.

Help me! **Saedni!**
Call a doctor **Ottlub daktour**

## L

## LANGUAGE

Arabic is the official language across the peninsula, but English is widely understood. Road signs are often in both languages. Large numbers of immigrant workers also speak Urdu, Hindi and other languages of the Indian subcontinent. In the hotels and resorts almost everything is conducted in both Arabic and English. Although English is widely understood, and Arabic is an extremely complex language to master, it always helps to learn a few basic words and phrases.

**Some useful Arabic words and phrases:**
yes/no **na'am/la**
hello/greeting **as-salam aleykum**
(response to hello) **wa-aleykum salam**
hello/welcome **ahlan wa sahlan/marhaba**
OK **tayib**
please **min fadlak**
thank you **shukran**
(response to thank you) **afwan**
how are you? **kaef halak?**
I am fine **Al-humdullilah**
good morning **sabah al-kher**
good evening **masa al-kher**
goodbye **ma'a salama/fi aman illah**
What is your name? **Shuw ismak?**
my name is... **ismi...**
I do not understand **Mabafahem**
Do you speak English? **Tetkallam inglizi?**
market **souq**
mosque **masjed**

## M

## MAPS

Maps are available for Old Muscat, Greater Muscat, Salalah and the whole of Oman. Several useful maps are published by the Ministry of Tourism, including *Sultanate of Oman*, *Muscat City*, *Governorate of Dhofar* and *Salalah*. They are free of charge but not that easy to obtain – try the overseas tourist offices or larger tour agencies. The *Sultanate of Oman Map* has useful city and regional maps included and can sometimes be found for sale in travel bookshops and online. Make sure you get the most up-to-date version. Explorer Publishing have several maps, including the useful *Muscat Map*.

## MEDIA

There are several English-language daily newspapers on sale at petrol stations and shops. The *Oman Daily Observer* (omanobserver. om) has good international coverage and is also available online. The *Times of Oman* (www.timesofoman.com) is similar to the *Oman Tribune* (www.omantribune.com). The *Muscat Daily* (www.muscat daily.com) is the fourth English paper with a focus on local news. *The Week* (www.theweek.co.om) comes out every Wednesday with good lifestyle information and listings. *Hi!* is a free weekly listings magazine and *Black and White* (www.blackandwhiteoman.com) is a free fortnightly magazine covering the arts, lifestyle and current affairs. The quarterly *Time Out Muscat* is also worth a read.

Most hotels and homes are fitted with satellite receivers and offer hundreds of channels. Sports channels show live events from around the world, including the English Premier League. Oman TV is the national television channel broadcaster but is essentially an Arabic-language station. Radio Sultanate of Oman at 90.4 FM is a mix of music, news and arts. Hi FM (www.hifmradio.com) is a Western-style pop station at 95.9 FM. BBC World Service broadcasting in English is on medium wave.

## MONEY

The Omani Rial (indicated as RO or OR) can be purchased overseas and brought into the country. One Rial is split into 1,000 Baisa, so that 1.5 RO will often be written as 1,500. Currency notes are 50, 20, 10, 5, 1, 0.5 RO, 200 and 100 Baisa, below which are coins for 50, 10 and 5 Baisa. The currency is linked to the US dollar and fluctuates slightly against other major currencies. Credit cards are widely accepted, and there are many ATM machines for withdrawing cash. Most shopping malls have efficient money exchanges, offering good rates, and are open much longer than banks. Hotels usually offer poorer exchange rates. Oman UAE Exchange (www.omanuaeexchange.com) has dozens of outlets.

## O

## OPENING TIMES

Bear in mind that there are no standard opening times and the following are a guideline only. Hours of private-sector businesses vary widely. Public organisations and businesses are open weekdays, which are officially Sun–Thu.

**Banks:** Generally Sun–Thu 8am–2pm; some branches have extended opening hours in the afternoon.

**Business:** Sun–Thu 8am–1pm and 4–7pm.

**Government offices:** Sun–Thu 7.30am–2.30pm; shorter hours during Ramadan.

**Shopping malls:** daily 9am–10pm (or midnight).

**Smaller shops:** Generally 9am–10pm (Fri until 4pm) but often closed afternoons.

**Museums:** See www.omantourism.gov.om for opening times.

## P

## PHOTOGRAPHY

Oman offers great opportunities for the keen photographer, with dramatic coastlines, mountains, architecture, bustling markets and friendly locals. Take plenty of memory cards or films, as local supplies are limited to popular types. Always ask before taking photos of people and respect their wishes, especially women. Do not photograph police, airports, harbours, military buildings or army personnel. Digital photo shops can quickly download photographs onto disk and print pictures. For technical help, quality photographic supplies and repairs, contact Paresh Shah at Shah Nagardas Manji & Co. (tel: +968 2470 2772), located opposite the bus station in Ruwi.

## POLICE

Traffic police enforce zero tolerance for drink-driving. After any accident or incident call the relevant ROP number (see page 120). Reporting a crime or theft can be time-consuming due to the paperwork involved, but you will always be courteously processed through the system.

## POST OFFICES

Oman's post offices are generally open Sun–Thu 8am–1.30pm. Main post offices may open longer. All incoming mail is collected from post-office boxes. Stamps can be bought from post offices and some shops.

## PUBLIC HOLIDAYS

There are two types of official holidays when government offices and banks are closed, secular (fixed) and religious (variable dates). Islamic dates move forward roughly 11 days every year with the Islamic calendar, which is a lunar calendar. For most people, Friday is a weekly holiday.

The fixed holidays are:

**1 January** New Year's Day

**23 July** Renaissance Day

**18–19 November** Oman National Day and HM Sultan Qaboos's birthday (the date of this holiday sometimes changes)

Oman's variable holidays change with the Islamic calendar:

*Al Hijra* Islamic New Year

*12 Rabiul Awal* Birthday of Prophet Muhammad

*Lailat al Miraj* The Prophet Muhammad's ascension

*Eid al Fitr* (The Minor Feast) celebrates the end of Ramadan (a few days)

*Eid al Adha* (The Grand Feast) commemorates the sacrifice of Abraham (a few days)

## PUBLIC TRANSPORT

**Taxis:** The best way to get around the towns is in an official taxi. There are fixed prices from the airports, otherwise negotiate and agree the price before getting in. Obtain information about local landmarks, as most taxi drivers have limited knowledge and can struggle to find the right address. Hotels and restaurants can arrange taxis for you.

**City minibuses:** Minibuses link the major centres and main road intersections around Greater Muscat, but are predominantly used by contract workers.

**Intercity buses:** The main bus station is in Ruwi centre, from where the Oman National Transport Company operates buses to a number of towns within Oman as well as to Dubai and Abu Dhabi. There are daily services to Sohar, taking 2.5 hours (then on to Buraymi); to Sur via Ibra (4.5 hours); to Salalah (13 hours) and to Nizwa (2.5 hours). For updated routes and timetables, tel: +968 2470 8522.

**Ferries:** A high-speed ferry service runs between Muscat and Khasab in Musandam twice weekly. Sometimes cancelled due to high seas or bad weather. There are more connections from Khasab to Shinas and Lima. For details and current schedules, visit www.nfc.om.

## R

## RELIGION

Islam is the official religion. Omanis and most imported workers are

Muslims, observing Islamic traditions and practices. The branch of Islam for most Omanis is Ibadism, with adherents also in East Africa, Libya, Tunisia and Algeria. Friday is the holy day of the week when the majority of shops and businesses close, at least in the morning. Non-Muslims cannot visit mosques, apart from the Sultan Qaboos Grand Mosque, which encourages everyone to learn more about Islam.

Many non-Muslims work in Oman and are free to worship at their own services. Just across the main road from the Al Falaj Hotel in Ruwi is the Catholic Church of St Peter and St Paul (tel: +968 2470 1893; ruwiparish.org), with English masses at 6am and 7pm, and extra services on weekends. Next door is a Hindu temple.

## T

## TELEPHONE

The international code for all Oman is +968, and mobile phone coverage is very good. Using your mobile phone (GSM) from overseas can be expensive due to high roaming charges via companies Ooredoo (tel: +968 9501 1500; www.ooredoo.om) and Omantel, (tel: +968 2424 1234; www.omantel.om).Buying a local SIM card (with a local Omani number) is a good idea for cheaper rates. To get a local mobile number, take your phone and passport to any telephone shop and get a 'pay as you go' deal. Credit is recharged using scratch cards bought from shops, petrol stations and online. All hotels offer direct-dial international services from your room, but these can be expensive.

## TIME ZONES

Oman is four hours ahead of GMT, with no daylight-saving time.

| New York | London | **Oman** | Sydney | Auckland |
| --- | --- | --- | --- | --- |
| 3am | 8am | **noon** | 5pm | 7pm |

## TIPPING

Service fees are included on receipts at most hotels, restaurants and bars, so any tip is additional. If somebody has done a good job or provided great service then it is usual to offer them a tip – waiters and bar staff (perhaps 10 percent), hotel staff, porters (0.5–1 RO) and attendants at service stations (0.2–0.5 RO). Taxi drivers do not expect a tip.

## TOILETS

There is a regular system of public toilets signposted along the main roads and in most towns and cities. It is generally no problem using the toilets of any restaurant, coffee shop, hotel or service station. Carrying tissues or toilet paper is a good idea.

Where is the toilet? **Wayn al-hammam?**

## TOURIST INFORMATION

**UK:** The Oman Ministry of Tourism is represented by Representation Plus (tel: +968 020-8877 4500; www.representationplus.co.uk).
**Head Office:** Ministry of Tourism, PO Box 200, Madinat as Sultan Qaboos, Muscat; www.omantourism.gov.om. Tourist information call centre, tel: +968 8007 7799. A small tourist desk sometimes supplies maps and leaflets at arrivals at Muscat International Airport, otherwise try hotels and tour agencies.

## V

## VISAS AND ENTRY REQUIREMENTS

To enter Oman, tourist/business visas are required by all nationalities (except other GCC states), and passports must be valid for a minimum of six months. Visitors from European Community countries plus the USA, Canada, Australia and New Zealand can purchase different kinds of visa on arrival at any airport, port or land border. A 10-day visa costs 5 RO. For details and fees for other visas, visit www.rop.gov.om. A one-year multiple-entry visa is also available, but each entry is only valid for 21 days, and passports must be valid for at least 12 months. The 24-hour transit visa for onward flights is free. For a small fee there is also a 72-hour transit visa – a useful way to see the highlights of Muscat between connecting flights. Visa requirements can change, so check with any tour agency or visa specialist such as Travcour (www.travcour.com).

Oman and Dubai operate a common visa facility. This means visitors who already have a valid visa for Dubai do not need to get a separate visa for Oman.

Penalties for attempting to import illegal drugs are severe, and there are also bans on some prescription drugs that might be sold legally in other countries. For more information on banned and restricted materials, visit www.omanairports.com/customsregulations.asp.

## W

## WEBSITES AND INTERNET CAFÉS

All towns and suburbs have internet cafés, often open after midnight. Internet business centres are found at all hotels, with many rooms and some coffee shops having Wi-Fi connections. When noting local web addresses, remember that some are '.om' as well as '.com'. Operating websites in Oman can be difficult due to restrictive bandwidths and slow speeds.

Tourist information:

www.omantourism.gov.om Government tourist website.

www.omanvisitors.com General tourism.

www.omanet.om Ministry of Information.

www.nizwa.net Nizwa and national information.

www.expatarrivals.com/oman/moving-to-oman General information for expats moving to Oman.

www.omaninfo.com Tourist and business information.

www.destinationoman.com General tourism.

www.oman.om Gateway to government information and eServices.

Oman information:

www.oman.org Oman Studies Centre, with links to many other sites.

www.oman.org.uk Anglo-Omani Society.

www.al-bab.com Gateway to the Arab world.

Official external sites:

www.fco.gov.uk UK Foreign and Commonwealth Office.

www.ukinoman.fco.gov.uk British Embassy in Oman.

www.britishcouncil.om/en British Council in Oman.

http://rs6.loc.gov/frd/cs/omtoc.html US Library of Congress country study.

# RECOMMENDED HOTELS

Oman maintains a high quality of hotels, almost all of which can be recommended. They are expensive compared to other Middle Eastern countries, but comparable to neighbouring Abu Dhabi. There is a lack of good hotels under 25 RO per night, but good smaller hotels are appearing around the country. At the top end are some of the most luxurious hotels in the world, whose rack rates quoted below are often negotiable. Check if the advertised price includes the 9 percent taxes and 8 percent service charge.

Rates at the same hotel vary throughout the year, and there are amazing discounted deals to be had during the low May–September season (apart from Dhofar), but it can be very hot outside! Better deals or upgrades are possible if you are a member of that hotel's frequent-stay programme, so try to join beforehand. Also enquire about special packages with flight and hotel included or other special offers, such as three-for-two-night deals. For longer stays or as an alternative to hotels there are some serviced apartments. In Dhofar, the appearance of the cooling *khareef* monsoon creates a peak period between June and September, when it is advisable to book well ahead.

Unless stated, all hotels provide restaurants, bar, pool, gift shop, info desk, spa, gym, satellite TV and internet access. The prices below are for a double room, including breakfast and government taxes.

| | |
|---|---|
| $$$$$ | over 150 RO |
| $$$$ | 100–150 RO |
| $$$ | 60–100 RO |
| $$ | 35–60 RO |
| $ | up to 35 RO |

## MUSCAT

**Al Bustan Palace $$$$$** *Al Bustan Street, Muscat, tel: +968 2479 9666, www.ritzcarlton.com.* The sumptuous Al Bustan helped put Muscat and

Oman on the map over 20 years ago, when it was originally built to accommodate official guests of the Sultan. Beautifully refurbished and with superb facilities, it is regularly voted one of the top hotels in the Middle East. Set in its own bay just outside Muscat.

**Al Falaj Hotel $$$** *1692 Al Hamriya, Ruwi, Muscat, tel: +968 2470 2311,* www.alfalajhotel.com. One of the oldest hotels in the country, now renewed, the Al Falaj is well located. Ideal for Ruwi, the Central Business District and the National Museum. Lively nightlife, with The Pub and the Souq Café, it also offers a Japanese restaurant, and good sporting facilities. Functional.

**Bowshar International $$$** *Sultan Qaboos Street, Al Ghubrah Junction, Muscat, tel: +968 2449 1105,* www.bowsharhotel.com. Affordable three-star hotel, with 38 rooms and a 24-hour restaurant with plenty of other choices and shops nearby. Ideal location between the airport and Ruwi/Mutrah.

**Chedi Hotel $$$$$** *PO Box 964, Al Khuwayr, Muscat, tel: +968 2452 4400,* www.ghmhotels.com/en/muscat. The GHM group, strong in Southeast Asia, has brought more top quality into Muscat with this oasis of peace and tranquillity. A blending of Arabian architecture with Asian design gives it a simple elegance that is incredibly calming. A choice of 60 standard and 52 deluxe rooms, all oozing beach-side style and luxury, with tranquil water features and two pools.

**Crowne Plaza $$$$–$$$$$** *PO Box 1445, Ruwi, tel: +968 2466 0660,* www.crowneplaza.com. Fabulous location at the end of Qurm Natural Park beside the sea. Fine dining and buffet restaurants with outdoor terraces overlooking pool and beach. Two bars including the Duke's Bar which is popular for TV coverage of sporting events and live music.

**Grand Hyatt $$$$$** *PO Box 951, Shati al Qurm, tel: +968 2464 1234,* www.muscat.grand.hyatt.com. Lavish five-star hotel which combines the needs of both business and tourist visitors. Located near the Diplomatic Area, the hotel surrounds its pools and opens out to the sea. The excellent amenities include a gym and a beauty salon, while dining options include the Safari Rooftop Grill, and Arabic and Italian restaurants.

**Majan Continental $$$** *PO Box 311, Al Ghubrah Street, Muscat, tel: +968 2422 1100, www.majanhotel.com.* Large 165-room hotel 2km (1.25 miles) from Sultan Qaboos Grand Mosque. Small three-storey block surrounding pool and villas. Fitness suite and spa. Lively nightlife with two nightclubs and bars. Good service and food. Complimentary airport transfer.

**Midan Hotel Suites $$$** *PO Box 1359, Al Marefah Street, Al Ghubrah, Muscat, tel: +968 2449 9787, www.midanoman.com.* This hotel offers 36 clean and modern suites with living room and kitchen. The Basil Thai restaurant is worth a try. Good value for money compared to other luxury hotels. Friendly staff and owner.

**Muscat Dune $$** *PO Box 2061, Al Maha Street, Al Khuwair, Muscat, tel: +968 2439 7500, www.muscatduneshotel.com.* Good location not far from the city centre. Spacious rooms offer splendid views over the sand dunes and mountains. Facilities include a rooftop swimming pool and gym. A good budget option by Omani standards.

**Park Inn by Radisson $$$$** *PO Box 1635, Al Khuwair, Muscat, tel: +968 2450 7888, www.parkinn.com/hotel-muscat.* 173 rooms just off the highway running through Al Ghubrah. The seventh-floor Sama Terrazza rooftop lounge is fabulous, with pool, bar, great views and live music, usually at weekends.

**Ramee Guestline Hotel $$–$$$** *PO Box 594, Qurm, Muscat, tel: +968 2456 4443, www.rameehotels.com.* Slightly hidden away, but still near to the beach and Qurm activities. 90 rooms over six floors around a small, shady pool. Great nightlife at the Rock Bottom Café, with nightly live bands and Friday DJ.

**Samara Hotel $$** *PO Box 525, Al Khuwair, Muscat, tel: +968 2448 1666, www.samarahoteloman.com.* Located in the heart of Al Khuwair and only 10 minutes' drive from the airport, this rather impersonal hotel offers 17 family and 63 single and double rooms. Clean and good value.

## NIZWA AND THE MOUNTAINS

### Nizwa

**Al Diyar Hotel $$** *PO Box 1166, Nizwa, tel: +968 2541 2402*, www.aldiyar hotel.com. Large hotel on the outskirts of Nizwa, popular with groups. 60 simple but spacious rooms set around a courtyard with swimming pool and games room. Nothing out of the ordinary, but good value.

**Falaj Daris $$$** *PO Box 312, Nizwa, tel: +968 2541 0500*, www.falajdaris hotel.com. Long-established low-rise hotel popular with groups, 4km (2.5 miles) from the town centre. Fifty-five rooms are set around two pools and gardens overlooking the mountains.

**Alila Jabal Akhdar $$$$** *Plot No 4 Al Roose, Nizwa, tel: +968 2534 4200*, www.alilahotels.com/jabalakhdar. High in the Al Hajar range, this mountain top oasis is a unique resort perfect for those looking to beat the desert heat and witness stunning views.

### Al Hamra region

**Al Hoota Rest House $$** *PO Box 1701, Birkat Al Sharaf, tel: +968 9282 8873*, www.alhootaresthouse.com. Just below Sharaf al Alameyn pass at the top of the Jabal al Akhdar Mountains. 20 simple rooms and some villas; the accommodation is clean and comfortable. The guesthouse is popular with trekking Europeans and 4x4 explorers during the winter months, and with locals escaping the heat in the summer.

**Ibri Oasis Hotel $$** *PO Box 387, Ibri, tel: +968 2569 6172/173/174*, email: ibrioasis@gmail.com. Friendly two-star hotel near the stadium 12km (7.5 miles) outside the town centre on the main road to Buraymi. 25 large rooms in a spacious hotel with adequate restaurant. No pool, gym or internet.

**Jibreen Hotel $$** *Jabrin Road, Bahla, tel: +968 2536 3340*, www.jibren hotel.com. Friendly hotel, just beyond left turn to Jabrin from Bahla, catering for visitors exploring the Nizwa region. 37 simple rooms and a restaurant in five-floor block. Free Wi-Fi and parking. Slightly over-priced, breakfast included.

# SOHAR AND BATINAH COAST

## Sohar

**Butterfly Hotel Suites $$–$$$** *PO Box 2452, Sultan Qaboos Road, Sohar, tel: +968 2684 3501, www.butterflyoman.com.* Part of a small chain of new hotels spread around Oman. 42 one- and two-bedroom suites, all equipped with kitchenette, refrigerator, microwave, washing machine and Wi-Fi, some overlooking the sea. Indoor pool with adjoining Africa Coffee House and Restaurant, next door to the Sohar Beach Hotel. A good option for the area.

**Crowne Plaza $$$$–$$$$$** *Falaj al Qabael, PO Box 478, Sohar 332, tel: +968 2685 0850, www.crowneplaza.com.* Inland from the Falaj al Qubail roundabout on the outskirts of Sohar is the luxurious Crowne Plaza hotel, temporary home for many of the expat managers at the port economic zone. More for business than tourism, this large hotel of 126 rooms is quiet through the day and lively at night. Features a four-lane bowling alley and lively Sports Bar with international TV coverage.

**Sohar Beach Hotel $$$** *PO Box 122, Al Tareef, Sohar, tel: +968 2684 1111, www.soharbeach.com.* Resembling a traditional Omani fort, this has been the beach resort of choice for almost 20 years, midway between Muscat and Dubai/Abu Dhabi. 45 rooms set around a pleasant open pool area and gardens. Good place to relax in peaceful surroundings. Tennis court, gym, bars, disco and lounge if you wish.

## Batinah Coast

**Al Sawadi Beach Resort $$$$** *PO Box 747, Barka, tel: +968 2679 5545.* Spacious beach complex built in 1997, about a 45-minute drive north of Muscat. Good for families and watersports fans. Kiteboarding and div-ing are the main attractions. The beautiful dive sites of the Daymaniyat Islands are just a boat ride away. 100 rooms with sea or garden view in a relaxing location, but quite expensive for what you get. Breakfast and dinner buffet.

## SUR AND THE EAST
### Sur

**Al-Ayjah Plaza $$** *PO Box 221, Al Ayjah, Sur, tel: +968 2554 4433,* www.al ayjahplazahotel.com. Relatively new hotel, about 5km (3 miles) from the centre of Sur, on the road to Ras al Hadd. 41 bright, open rooms – request one with a sea view balcony. Great Turkish restaurant with *shisha*. Good option for visiting Turtle Reserve.

**Sur Hotel $** *PO Box 299, Sur, tel: +968 9556 6809,* www.surhotel.net. 31 clean rooms in the centre of the Old Town. No restaurant but local eateries nearby. Good budget choice.

**Sur Plaza $$$** *PO Box 908, Sur, tel: +968 2554 3777,* www.omanhotels. com. Four-storey hotel with 92 rooms on the main road into Sur. Three bars, the Captain's pub and 'Oysters' restaurant overlooking pool area.

### The East Coast

**Ras al Hadd Beach Hotel $$** *PO Box 400, Ras al Hadd, tel: +968 2556 9111,* www.surhotelsoman.com. Operated by Mubarak Juma Bahwan Group mid-priced hotel in a remote location 60km (37 miles) east of Sur. Beachside location and a good base for turtle-watching.

**Ras al Jinz Turtle Reserve $$$** *Ras al Jinz, tel: +968 9655 0606/0707,* www.rasaljinz-turtlereserve.com. This eco-tourism project provides the best turtle-watching experience. Having a room at the reserve centre guarantees your free places on the guided night and early morning visits. 31 rooms, including 17 twin en suite rooms and 12 eco tents. It's advisable to book well in advance.

**Turtle Beach Resort $$** *PO Box 303, Ras al Hadd, tel: +968 2553 3300.* Collection of beach-side cabins with walls covered with date palm leaves.

Some are really basic while others boast air condition, TV, fridge and bathrooms. Quite expensive for a grade above camping. The resort offers outdoor sport activities such as kayaking, snorkelling, fishing trips and turtle-watching, as well as indoor sports, including basketball, billiards and darts. Cash only.

## SALALAH AND DHOFAR

**Beach Villas $** *PO Box 20, Al Dahariz, Salalah 214, tel: +968 2323 5999*, www.beach-villas-salalah.com. A few hundred metres east of the Crowne Plaza Hotel, this small, family-run hotel is right on the beach. Easy-going atmosphere with small pool and restaurant. Rooms on the front look out to sea. Owners can arrange guides, tours and car rental. Extremely popular; the quietest period is Apr–June. Cash only.

**Crowne Plaza Resort $$$$–$$$$$** *PO Box 870, Salalah 211, tel: +968 2323 8000*, www.crowneplaza.com. Large hotel complex in a superb beach-front location, 5km (3 miles) east along the coast from central Salalah. Choice of three restaurants, and the English-style pub and Al Luban nightclub make it a popular nightspot. The dive centre is run by Extra Divers.

**Haffa House Hotel $$** *PO Box 427, Salalah 211, tel: +968 2329 5444*, www.shanfarihotels.com. Run by the large Shanfari Group. 60 large rooms and 63 flats in tower block with a swimming pool and gym. Well located at the end of the airport road. Shanfari also run the nearby Samharam Tourist Village ($$$) on the beach close to the Hilton Resort.

**Hamdan Plaza Hotel $$$** *PO Box 2498, Salalah 211, tel: +968 2321 1024*, www.hamdanplazahotel.com. Large facade above a row of shops opposite Lulu hypermarket. On the corner of the main ring road from the airport, and the Itin Road to Job's Tomb. 18-year-old building with 186 rooms, all huge, with a big pool and choice of Chinese and international restaurants. Very popular during *khareef* summer season.

**Hilton Salalah Resort $$$$–$$$$$** *PO Box 699, Salalah 211, tel: +968 2313 3333*, www3.hilton.com. Well-established hotel in a beautiful beach-side location among lush palm groves. The 147 rooms are spread among low-rise buildings, with spacious pool, garden, beach areas and dive centre. Focus for much of the nightly entertainment in Salalah, with choice of six restaurants and bars. The Al Maha terrace restaurant overlooks the pool and gardens, while the open-air Palm Grove boasts a delightful setting by the Indian Ocean.

**Salalah Plaza Hotel $$** *Auqad, PO Box 480, Salalah 217, tel: +968 2321 0794.* This centrally located hotel offers clean rooms with all modern amenities and free Wi-Fi. Breakfast is included in the price. Good value.

# MUSANDAM

**Atana Khasab $$$** *PO Box 434, Khasab, tel: +968 2673 0777, www.atana hotels.com.* Wonderfully located on a low headland surrounded by the sea. Each of the 60 rooms has its own private terrace or balcony over-looking the sea. Restaurant, lounge, 'Darts Bar' English pub and oriental tent for coffee and *shisha* smoking. Good-quality dive centre and shop run by Extra Divers (www.extradivers-worldwide.com). The hotel can also arrange boat trips, mountain safaris and Zaree trips offered by a group of local women focusing on the art of henna design, traditional costume and local cuisine. There is also a Golden Tulip hotel (www.goldentulip. com) in Daba (or Dibba), the southern entry point to the peninsula.

**Khasab Hotel $$** *PO Box 111, Khasab, tel: +968 2673 0267, www.khasab hotel.net.* Located on the main road south of town beside the airport. 42 rooms in the main building set beside a tree-lined pool. Restaurant open for breakfast, lunch and dinner which can be taken indoors or poolside. Cash only. Offers a variety of boat and diving trips and sight-seeing tours, organised through its sister company, Dolphin Tours (www.dolphintour.net).

**Six Senses $$$$$** *PO Box 212, Dibba, Musandam, tel: +968 2673 5555, www.sixsenses.com.* A very secluded, high-end resort set in the pictur-esque Zighy Bay. The 82 villas are strung in isolated luxury along its own mile-long beach. Fabulous food, Zen spa, and a whole host of facilities, this is the perfect place for a romantic hideaway. Only 90 minutes' drive from Dubai – you can even opt to arrive by paraglider.

# DICTIONARY

## ENGLISH – ARABIC

**adj** adjective     **adv** adverb     **BE** British English     **n** noun     **prep** preposition     **v** verb

### A

**accept** يقبل yaqbal
**access** مدخل madkhal
**access** v **(internet)** يدخل yadkhul
**accident** حادث Haadith
**accompany** يرافق yuraafiq
**account** حساب Hisaab
**acetaminophen** سيتامول seetaamool
**acupuncture** علاج بالإبر ʻilaaj bil-ibar
**adapter** محوّل muHawwil
**address** عنوان ʻunwaan
**admission** رسم الدخول **(to museum etc)** rasm ad-dukhool
**after** بعد baʻad
**afternoon** بعد الظهر baʻad aZ-Zuhr
**aftershave** عطر بعد الحلاقة ʻuTr baʻad al-Halaaqa
**age** عمر ʻumr
**agency** وكالة wakaala
**AIDS** أيدز aydz
**air conditioner** مكيف الهواء mukayyif al-hawaa
**airline** خطوط جوية khuTooT jaweeya
**airplane** طائرة Taaʼira
**airport** مطار maTaar
**air pump** منفاخ minfaakh
**aisle seat** مقعد على الممشى maqʻad ʻala al-mamsha
**Algeria** الجزائر al-jazaaʼir
**Algerian** جزائري jazaaʼiree
**allergic** يعاني من الحساسية yuʻaanee min al-Hasaaseeya
**allowe** مسموح masmooH
**alone** بمفرده bi-munfaridih
**alter** يعدل yuʻaddil
**alternate route** طريق آخر Tareeq aakhar
**aluminum foil** رقائق المنيوم raqaaʼiq aluminyoom
**amazing** مدهش mud-hish
**ambulance** سيارة الإسعاف sayaarat al-isʼaaf
**American** adj أمريكي amreekee

**amusement park** مدينة الملاهي madeenat al-malaahee
**anemic** مصاب بفقر الدم muSaab bi-fuqr ad-damm
**anesthesia** تخدير takhdeer
**animal** حيوان Haywaan
**ankle** كاحل kaaHil
**another** آخر aakhar
**antibiotics** المضادات الحيوية muDadaat al-Hayawaya
**antiques store** محل الأنتيكات maHal al-anteekaat
**antiseptic cream** كريم معقم kreem muʻaqim
**anything** أي شيء ay shay
**apartment** شقة shiqqa
**appendix** الزائدة الدودية az-zaaʼidat ad-doodeeya
**appointment** موعد mawʻid
**Arab** **(person)** عربي ʻarabee
**Arabic** adj عربي ʻarabee; n **(language)** العربية al-ʻarabeeya
**arcade** قاعة الألعاب qaaʻat al-alʻaab
**area code** رمز المنطقة ramz al-manTaqa
**arm** ذراع dhiraaʼ
**aromatherapy** علاج أروماتي ʻilaaj aroomaatee
**arrivals (airport)** الوصول al-wuSool
**arrive** يصل yaSil
**arthritis** التهاب مفاصل iltihaab mafaaSil
**aspirin** أسبرين asbireen
**assistance** مساعدة musaaʻada
**asthmatic** مريض بالربو mareeD bir-rabu
**ATM** الصراف الآلي aS-Saraaf al-aalee
**attack (on person)** اعتداء iʻtidaaʼ
**attraction (sightseeing)** المعلم الرئيسية al-maʻallim ar-raʼeeseeya
**attractive (person)** جذاب jadhaab
**Australia** أستراليا ustraaleeyaa
**Australian** أسترالي ustraalee
**automatic** أوتوماتيكي awtoomaateekee
**available** غير مشغول ghayr mashghool

## B

**baby** رضيع raDee'
**baby bottle** رضاعة riDaa'a
**baby food** طعام للرضع Ta'aam lir-raDa'
**babysitter** مربية أطفال murabeeyat aTfaal
**baby wipe** محارم للطفل maHaarim liT-Tifl
**back (of body)** ظهر Zuhr
**backache** ألم في الظهر alam fee iZ-Zuhr
**backpack** حقيبة ظهر Haqeeba Zuhr
**bad** ردي' radee'
**bag** كيس kees
**baggage claim** استلام الحقائب istilaam al-Haqaa'ib
**Bahrain** البحرين al-baHrayn
**Bahraini** بحريني baHraynee
**bakery** المخبز al-makhbaz
**ballet** عرض باليه 'arD baalayh
**bandage** ضمادات Damaadaat
**ban** بنك bank
**bar** بار baar
**barber** حلاق رجالي Halaaq rijaalee
**baseball** البيسبول al-baysbool
**basket** سلة silla
**basketball** كرة السلة kurrat as-silla
**bathroom** حمام Hamaam
**battery** بطارية baTaareeya
**be** يكون yakoon
**beach** شاطيء shaaTee'
**beautiful** جميل jameel
**bed** سرير sareer
**before** قبل qabl
**begin** يبدأ yabda'
**beginner** مبتدىء mubtadi'
**behind** خلف khalf
**beige** بيج bayj
**belt** حزام Hizaam
**best** الأحسن al-aHsan
**bet** n مراهنة muraahana
**better** أفضل afDal
**bicycle** دراجة daraaja
**big** كبير kabeer
**bikini wax** شمع خط البيكيني shama' khaT al-beekeenee
**bill** n حساب Hisaab
**bird** طير Tayr
**birthday** عيد ميلاد 'eed meelaad
**black** أسود aswad

**bladder** مثانة mathaana
**blanket** بطانية baTaaneeya
**bleed** ينزف yanzif
**blender** خلاط khalaaT
**blood** دم damm
**blood pressure** ضغط الدم DaghuT ad-damm
**blouse** بلوزة blooza
**blue** أزرق azraq
**boarding pass** بطاقة صعود biTaaqat Su'ood
**boat** قارب qaarib
**boat trip** رحلة بالقارب riHla bil-qaarib
**bone** عظم 'aZm
**book** كتاب kitaab
**bookstore** مكتبة maktaba
**boot** جزمة jazma
**boring** ممل mumill
**botanical garden** حديقة النباتات Hadeeqat an-nabaataat
**bottle** زجاجة zujaaja
**bottle opener** فتاحة زجاجات fataaHa zujaajaat
**bowl** زبدية zubdeeya
**box** علبة 'ulba
**boxing** ملاكمة mulaakama
**boy** صبي Sabee
**boyfriend** صاحب SaaHib
**bra** حمالة صدر Hamaala Sadr
**bracelet** سوار siwaar
**brake** فرامل faraamil
**break (tooth, bone)** يكسر yukassir
**breakdown** تعطل ta'Tul
**breakfast** فطور fuToor
**break-in** اقتحام iqtiHaam
**breast** ثدي thaddee
**breastfeed** ترضع turaDDi'
**breath** يتنفس yatanaffas
**bridge** جسر jisr
**briefs** سروال داخلي sirwaal daakhilee
**bring** يجلب yajlib
**British** adj بريطاني breeTaanee
**broken** مكسور maksoor
**brooch** بروش broosh
**broom** مكنسة miknasa
**brother** أخ akh
**brown** بني bunnee
**bugs** حشرات Hasharaat
**building** مبنى mabna

**burn** n حرق Harq
**bus** باص baaS
**bus station** محطة الباص maHaTat al-baaS
**bus stop** موقف الباص mawqif al-baaS
**bus ticket** تذكرة للباص tadhkara lil-baaS
**bus tour** جولة بالباص jawla bil-baaS
**business** أعمال a'maal
**business card** كرت الأعمال kart al-a'maal
**business center** مركز الأعمال markaz al-a'maal
**business class** درجة الأعمال darajat al-a'maal
**business hours** أوقات العمل awqaat al-'amal
**busy** مشغول mashghool
**butcher** لحام laHaam
**butter** زبدة zibda
**buttock** ردفين ridfayn
**buy** v يشتري yashtaree
**bye** مع السلامة ma' as-salaama

## C

**cabin** كابينة kaabeena
**cafe** مقهى maqha
**call (telephone)** يتصل yattaSil
**call collect** كلفة المكالمة على المتصل kulfat al-mukaalama 'ala al-muttaSil
**calorie** حريرات Hurayraat
**camera** كاميرا kaameeraa
**camera store** محل الكاميرات maHal al-kaameeraat
**camp** v يخيم yukhayyam
**camping stove** فرن مخيم furn mukhayyam
**campsite** مخيم mukhayyam
**Canada** كندا kanadaa
**Canadian** كندي kanadee
**cancel** ألغي alghee
**car** سيارة sayaara
**car hire [BE]** تأجير السيارات ta'jeer as-sayaaraat
**car park [BE]** موقف السيارات mawqif as-sayaaraat
**car rental** تأجير السيارات ta'jeer as-sayaaraat
**car seat** مقعد سيارة maq'ad sayaara
**carafe** إبريق ibreeq
**card** بطاقة biTaaqa
**carry-on (piece of hand luggage)** حقيبة يد Haqeeba yad
**cart (for luggage, shopping)** عربة 'araba
**carton** كرتونة kartoona
**cash** كاش kaash
**cash advance** دفعة مسبقة duf'a musabbaqa

**cashier** محاسب muHaasib
**casino** كازينو kazeenoo
**castle** قلعة qal'a
**cave** كهف kahf
**CD** سي دي see dee
**cell phone** هاتف نقال haatif naqaal
**Celsius** سيلسيوس silseeyoos
**centimeter** سنتمتر centimeter
**certificate** شهادة shahaada
**chair** كرسي kursee
**change** v يغير حفاظ الطفل yughayir HifaaD aT-Tifl; v (money) يبدل yubaddil; v (travel) يغير yughayir
**charcoal** فحم faHm
**charge** v يطلب yaTlub; n (cost) سعر si'r
**cheap** رخيص rakheeS
**check (in restaurant)** حساب Hisaab; n (payment) يفحص yafHaS; n (luggage) شيك sheek; v يودع yuwadi' al-amti'a الأمتعة
**check-in** إجراءات السفر ijra'aat as-safar
**checking account** حساب الجاري Hisaab al-jaaree
**check-out (from hotel)** مغادرة الفندق mughaadarat al-funduq
**chemical toilet** تواليت كيميائي at-toowaaleet al-kimiyaa'ee
**chemist [BE]** صيدلية Saydleeya
**cheque [BE]** شيك sheek
**chest** صدر Sadr
**chest pain** ألم في الصدر alam fee iS-Sadr
**chewing gum** علكة 'ilka
**child** طفل Tifl
**children's menu** قائمة طعام للأطفال qaa'imat Ta'aam lil-aTfaal
**children's portion** وجبات أصغر للأطفال wajabaat aSghar lil-aTfaal
**child's seat** كرسي خاص للأطفال kursee khaaS lil-aTfaal
**chopstick** عيدان صينية للأكل 'eedaan Seeneeya lil-akul
**church** كنيسة kaneesa
**cigar** سيجار seegaar
**cigarette** سجائر sijaa'ir
**claim form** استمارة مطالبة istimaara muTaalaba
**class (in school)** صف Saff
**classical music** موسيقى كلاسيكية mooseeqa klaaseekeeya
**clean** adj نظيف naZeef
**cleaning supplies** مواد تنظيف mawaad tanZeef

**cliff** منحدر munHadar
**cling film [BE]** غلاف نايلون ghilaaf naayloon
**clock** ساعة حائطية saa'a Haa'iTeeya
**close (near)** قريب qareeb; v يغلق yaghliq
**closed** مغلق mughlaq
**clothes** ملابس malaabis
**clothing store** محل الملابس maHal al-malaabis
**club** نادي naadee
**coat** معطف mi'Taf
**coffee shop** مقهى maqha
**coin** قطعة نقدية qiT'a naqdeeya
**colander** مصفاة miSfaah
**cold** adj بارد baarid; n (illness) رشح rashH
**colleague** زميل zameel
**cologne** كولونيا kooloonyaa
**color** صبغة Sabgha
**comb** مشط mishT
**come** يأتي ya'tee
**complaint** شكوى shakwa
**computer** كومبيوتر kumbyootir
**concert** حفلة موسيقية Hafla mooseeqeeya
**concert hall** قاعة الحفلات الموسيقية qaa'at al-Haflaat al-mooseeqeeya
**conditioner** بلسم balsam
**condom** واقي ذكري waaqee dhikree
**conference** مؤتمر mu'tamar
**confirm** يؤكد yu'akid
**congestion** احتقان iHtiqaan
**connect** يتصل yuttaSil
**connection (travel)** تبديل طائرة tabdeel Taa'ira; (internet) اتصال ittiSaal
**constipated** مصاب بإمساك muSaab bi-imsaak
**consulate** قنصلية qunSuleeya
**consultant** مستشار mustashaar
**contact** v يتصل yuttaSil
**contact lens** عدسة لاصقة 'adasa laaSiqa
**contact lens solution** محلول للعدسات اللاصقة maHlool lil-'adasaat al-laaSiqa
**contagious** معد mu'din
**convention hall** قاعة المؤتمرات qaa'at al-mu'tamaraat
**cook** v يطبخ yaTbukh
**cooking facilities** لوازم طبخ lawaazim Tabkh
**cooking gas** غاز الطبخ ghaaz aT-Tabkh
**cool (temperature)** بارد قليلاً baarid qaleelan
**copper** نحاس nuHaas
**corkscrew** فتاحة النبيذ fataaHat an-nabeedh

**corner** زاوية zaaweeya
**cost** v يكلف yukalif
**cot** سرير قابل للطوي sareer qaabil liT-Tawwi; [BE] سرير أطفال sareer aTfaal
**cotton** قطن quTn
**cough** n سعال su'aal
**country code** رمز البلد ramz al-balad
**cover charge** رسم الخدمة rasm al-khidma
**cramps** تشنج tashannuj
**crash (in car)** حادث اصطدام Haadith iSTidaam
**cream (ointment)** مرهم marham
**credit** ائتمان i'timaan
**credit card** بطاقة ائتمان biTaaqat al-i'timaan
**crew neck** ياقة مدورة yaaqa mudawwara
**crib** سرير أطفال sareer aTfaal
**crystal** كريستال kreestaal
**cup** فنجان finjaan
**currency** عملة 'umla
**currency exchange** تبديل العملات tabdeel al-'umlaat
**currency exchange office** مكتب تبديل العملات maktab tabdeel al-'umlaat
**customs** الجمرك al-jumruk
**customs declaration form** تصريح جمركي taSreeH jumrukee
**cut** n جرح jurH; v (hair) يقص yaquSS
**cute** جميل jameel
**cycling** ركوب الدراجة rukoob ad-daraaja

**D**

**dairy** منتجات الألبان muntajaat al-albaan
**damaged** تالف taalif
**dance** v يرقص yarquS
**dance club** نادي للرقص naadee lir-raqS
**dancing** الرقص ar-raqS
**dangerous** خطر KhaTeer
**dark** غامق ghaamik
**date (on calendar)** تاريخ ta'reekh
**day** يوم yawm
**deaf** أصم aSam
**debit** سحب من الحساب الجاري saHab min al-Hisaab al-jaaree
**deck chair** كرسي للشاطئ kursee lish-shaaTee'
**degrees (temperature)** درجات darajaat
**delay** n يتأخر yata'akhar
**delete** v يمحي yamHi

**delicatessen** محل الأطعمة الفاخرة maHal al-aT'imat al-faakhira

**delicious** لذيذ ladheedh

**denim** جينز jeenz

**dentist** طبيب أسنان Tabeeb asnaan

**deodorant** مزيل الرائحة muzeel ar-raa'iHa

**department store** محل تجاري maHal tijaaree

**departure gate** بوابات السفر bawaabaat as-safar

**departures (airport)** مغادرة mughaadara

**deposit** عربون 'arboon; **(at bank)** إيداع eedaa'

**desert** صحراء SaHraa'

**detergent** منظف munaZZif

**detour** تحويلة taHweela

**develop (film)** تحميض taHmeeD

**diabetic** مريض بالسكري mareeD bis-sukaree

**dial** v يضغط yiDghuT

**diamond** ألماس al-maas

**diaper** حفاظ HifaaZ

**diarrhea** إسهال is-haal

**diesel** ديزل deezil

**difficult** صعب Su'ub

**digital** ديجيتال dijeetaal

**digital camera** كاميرا ديجيتال kaameeraa dijeetaal

**digital photo** صور ديجيتال Suwwar dijeetaal

**digital print** صور ديجيتال Suwwar dijeetaal

**dining room** غرفة الطعام ghurfat aT-Ta'aam

**dinner** عشاء 'ashaa'

**direction** اتجاه itijaah

**dirty** وسخ wisikh

**disabled** معاق mu'aaq

**disabled-accessible [BE]** مكان مجهز لاستقبال المعاقين makaan mujahhaz li-istiqbaal al-mu'aaqeen

**disabled toilet [BE]** تواليت خاص للمعاقين toowaaleet khaaS lil-mu'aaqeen

**disconnect** يقطع الاتصال yaqTa' al-ittiSaal

**discount** تخفيض takhfeeD

**dish** صحن SaHn

**dishwasher** غسالة الصحون ghasaalat aS-SuHoon

**dishwashing liquid** سائل لغسيل الصحون saa'il li-ghaseel aS-SuHoon

**display case** فترينة fitreenaa

**disposable** موس الحلاقة للاستعمال مرة واحدة moos al-Halaaqa lil-isti'maal marra waaHida

**dive** v يغطس yaghTus

**diving equipment** معدات الغوص mu'iddaat lil-ghawS

**divorced** مطلق muTallaq

**dizzy** يشعر بدوار yash'ur bi-duwaar

**doctor** طبيب Tabeeb

**doll** دمية dumya

**dollar** دولار doolaar

**domestic** محلي maHalee

**door** باب baab

**dormitory** غرفة نوم ghurfa nawm

**double bed** سرير مزدوج sareer muzdawwaj

**double room** غرفة مزدوجة ghurfa muzdawwaja

**downtown (direction)** باتجاه مركز المدينة bi-ittijah markaz al-madeena

**downtown area** مركز المدينة markaz al-madeena

**dozen** دزينة duzeena

**dress (woman's)** فستان fustaan

**dress code** لباس مناسب libaas munaasib

**drink** n مشروب mashroob; v يشرب yashrab

**drinks menu** قائمة المشروبات qaa'imat al-mashrooobaat

**drive** v يقود yaqood

**driver's license** رخصة قيادة rukhSa qeeyaada

**drop (of liquid)** قطرة qaTra

**drowsiness** خمول khumool

**dry cleaner** محل تنظيف ألبسة maHal tanZeef albisa

**dummy [BE]** لهاية lahaaya

**during** خلال khilaal

**duty (customs)** رسوم rusoom

**duty-free goods** بضائع معفية من الضرائب biDaa'i' mu'feeya min aD-Daraa'ib

**DVD** دي في دي dee fee dee

## E

**ear** أذن udhn

**earache** ألم في الأذن alam fee il-udhn

**early** مبكر mubakkir

**earrings** حلق Halaq

**east** شرق sharq

**easy** سهل sahil

**eat** يأكل ya'kul

**economy class** درجة سياحية daraja seeyaaHeeya

**Egypt** مصر muSr

**Egyptian** مصري muSree

**elbow** مرفق mirfaq

**electric outlet** مأخذ كهرباء ma'khadh kahrabaa'

**elevator** مصعد miS'ad

**e-mail** بريد إلكتروني bareed iliktroonee

**e-mail address** عنوان الكتروني 'unwaan iliktroonee

emergency طوارىء Tawaari'
emergency exit مخرج الطوارئ makhraj aT-Tawaari'
empty adj فارغ faarigh
enamel (jewelry) خزف khazaf
end v ينتهي yantahee
engaged خاطب khaaTib
English (language) الانكليزية al-ingleezeeya
engrave ينقش yunqush
enjoy يستمتع yastamata'
enter يدخل yadkhul
entertainment تسلية tasleeya
entrance مدخل madkhal
envelope ظرف Zarf
epileptic مصاب بداء الصرع muSaab bidaa' aS-Sura'
equipment معدات mu'idaat
escalator سلالم كهربائية salaalim kahrabaa'eeya
e-ticket تذكرة الكترونية tadhkarat iliktrooneeya
e-ticket check-in إجراءات السفر للتذاكر الالكترونية ijraa'aat as-safar lit-tadhaakir al-iliktrooneeya
evening مساء masaa'
excess luggage وزن أمتعة زائد wazn amti'a zaa'id
exchange v يبدل yubaddil
exchange fee رسم الصرف rasm aS-Sarf
exchange rate سعر الصرف si'r aS-Sarf
excursion رحلة riHla
exhausted منهك munhak
exit v يخرج yakhruj; n خروج khurooj
expensive غالي ghaalee
experienced متمرس mutamarras
express سريع saree'
express bus باص سريع baaS saree'
express train قطار سريع qiTaar saree'
extension رقم فرعي raqm far'ee
extra إضافي iDaafee
extra large كبير جداً kabeer jiddan
extract v (tooth) يخلع yakhla'
eye عين 'ayn

F

face وجه wajah
facial n تنظيف الوجه tanZeef al-wajah
family عائلة 'aa'ila
fan (appliance) مروحة marwaHa
far بعيد ba'eed
farm مزرعة mazra'a
far-sighted مصاب بمد النظر muSaab bi-madd an-naZar

fast سريع saree'
fast-food place مطعم للوجبات السريعة maT'am lil-wajabaat as-saree'a
fat free خال من الدسم khaal min ad-dasm
father أب ab
fax فاكس faaks
fax number رقم الفاكس raqm al-faaks
fee رسم rasm
feed v (baby) يطعم yuT'im
ferry معدية mu'deeya
fever حرارة مرتفعة Haraara murtafi'a
field حقل Haql
fill out (form) يملأ yimlaa
fill up (tank) يملأ yimlaa
filling (in tooth) حشوة Hashwa
film (camera) فيلم feelm
fine (good) جيد jayyid; (for breaking law) مخالفة mukhaalafa
finger إصبع iSba'
fingernail ظفر Zifr
fire حريق Hareeq
fire department الإطفاء al-iTfaa'
fire door مخرج الحريق makhraj al-Hareeq
first أول awal
first class درجة أولى darajat oola
fit v (clothing) يقيس yaqees
fitting room غرفة القياس ghurfat al-qeeyaas
fix v يصلح yuSalliH
fixed-price سعر محدد si'r muHaddad
flashlight فلاش flaash
flash photography تصوير بالفلاش taSweer bil-flaash
flat (on vehicle) بنشر bunshur
flight رحلة جوية riHla jaweeya
floor (underfoot) أرض arD
florist محل الزهور maHal az-zuhoor
flower زهرة zahra
folk music الموسيقى الشعبية al-mooseeqa ash-sha'abeeya
food طعام Ta'aam
food processor فرامة faraama
foot قدم qadam
football [BE] كرة القدم kurrat al-qadam
for لـ li-
forecast توقعات الطقس tawqu'aat aT-Taqs
forest غابة ghaaba
fork شوكة shawka

form (to fill in) استمارة istimaara
formula (for baby) طعام للرضع Ta'aam lir-raDa'
fort حصن HiSn
fountain نافورة naafoora
free مجاني majaanee
freezer فريزر fireezir
friend صديق Sadeeq
from من min
frying pan مقلاة miqlaah
full-service خدمة كاملة khidma kaamila

## G

game لعبة lu'ba
garage جراج garaaj
garbage bag كيس قمامة kees qamaama
gas بنزين binzeen
gas station محطة البنزين maHaTat al-binzeen
gate (at airport) بوابة bawaaba
gel جل jil
generic drug دواء بدون علامة تجارية dawaa'
　bidooni 'alaama tijaareeya
get off (a train/bus/subway) ينزل yanzil
gift هدية hadeeya
gift shop محل الهدايا التذكارية maHal al-hadaayaa
　at-tidhkaareeya
girl بنت bint
girlfriend صاحبة SaaHiba
give يعطي ya'Tee
give way [BE] أعط أحقية الطريق a'aT aHaqeeyat
　aT-Tareeq
glass (for drink) كأس ka's; (material) زجاج zujaaj
glasses نظارات naZaaraat
go يذهب yadh-hab
gold ذهب dhahab
golf جولف golf
golf club مضارب غولف maDaarib golf
golf course أرض الغولف arD al-golf
good جيد jayyid
goodbye مع السلامة ma' as-salaama
good afternoon مساء الخير masaa' al-khayr
good evening مساء الخير masaa' al-khayr
good morning صباح الخير SabaaH al-khayr
gram غرام gram
grandchild حفيد Hafeed
grandparent جد jadd
gray رمادي ramaadee

green أخضر akhDar
grocery store محل الخضار maHal al-khuDaar
groundcloth حصيرة HaSeera
ground floor الطابق الأرضي aT-Taabiq al-arDee
ground-floor room غرفة في الطابق الأرضي ghurfa fee
　iT-Taabiq al-arDee
groundsheet [BE] حصيرة HaSeera
group مجموعة mujmoo'a
guide دليل daleel
guide (book) كتاب عن المكان kitaab 'an al-makaan
guide dog كلب إرشاد العميان kalb irshaad al-'umyaan
Gulf (Persian) الخليج العربي al-khaleej al-'arabee
gym جيمنازيوم jeemnaaziyoom
gynecologist طبيب نسائي Tabeeb nisaa'ee

## H

hair شعر sha'r
hairbrush فرشاة الشعر furshaat ash-sha'r
haircut قصة شعر qaSSa sha'r
hair dryer مجفف شعر mujaffif sha'r
hair salon صالون كوافير Saaloon koowaafeer
hairspray مثبت الشعر muthabbit ash-sha'r
hairstylist كوافير koowaafeer
half نصف nusf
half-kilo نصف كيلو nusf-kilo
hammer مطرقة miTraqa
hand يد yad
handbag [BE] حقيبة يد Haqeeba yad
hand luggage [BE] حقيبة يد Haqeeba yad
handicapped معاق mu'aaq
handicapped-accessible خاص للمعاقين khaaS
　lil-mu'aaqeen
happen يحصل yaHSal
happy سعيد sa'eed
hat قبعة qub'a
hay fever حمى القش Hummi il-qash
head رأس ra's
headache صداع Sudaa'
headphones سماعات samaa'aat
health صحة SiHHa
health food store محل الأطعمة الصحية maHal
　al-aT'imat aS-SiHHeeya
hearing impaired ضعيف سمعه sam'i Da'eef
heart قلب qalb
heart condition قصور في القلب quSoor fee il-qalb
heat الحر al-Hurr

heater سخان sakhaan
heating [BE] تدفئة tadfi'a
hello السلام عليكم as-salaam 'alaykum
helmet خوذة khoodha
help n مساعدة musaa'ada
here هنا huna
hi مرحبا marHaban
high عالي 'aalee
high blood pressure ضغط دم مرتفع DaghuT damm murtafi'
highchair كرسي عالي kursee 'aalin
highlights (in hair) هاي لايت haay laayt
highway الطريق السريع aT-Tareeq as-saree'
hiking boots جزمة مريحة للمشي jazma mareeHa lil-mashi
hill تل till
hire [BE] يستأجر yasta'jir
hire car [BE] سيارة مستأجرة sayaara musta'jara
hitchhike طلب توصيل Talb tawSeel
hold on (telephone) ينتظر yantaZir
holiday [BE] إجازة ijaaza
horsetrack طريق للخيول Tareeq lil-khuyool
hospital مستشفى mustashfa
hostel نزل nuzul
hot ساخن saakhin; (spicy) حار Haar
hotel فندق funduq
hour ساعة saa'a
house بيت bayt
housekeeping services خدمات تنظيف khidmaat tanZeef
how كيف kayf
how much كم الحساب kam al-Hisaab
hug v يعانق yu'aaniq
hungry جائع jaa'i'
hurt v يؤلم yu'alim
husband زوج zawj

**I**

ibuprofen إيبوبروفين eebooброofeen
ice machine ماكينة ثلج maakeena thalj
icy يوجد جليد yoojad jileed
ID هوية شخصية haweeya shakhSeeya
ill [BE] مريض mareeD
in fee
include يشمل yashmal
indoor pool مسبح مسقوف masbaH masqoof

inexpensive غير مكلف ghayr muklif
infected ملتهب multahib
information معلومات ma'loomaat
information desk استعلامات isti'lamaat
insect bite لدغة الحشرات ladghat al-Hasharaat
insect repellent مادة طاردة للحشرات maada Taarida lil-Hasharaat
insert v يدخل yadkhil
inside الداخل ad-daakhil
insomnia أرق araq
instant messenger ماسنجر maasinjar
insulin انسولين insooleen
insurance تأمين ta'meen
insurance card بطاقة تأمين biTaaqat ta'meen
insurance company شركة التأمين shirkat at-ta'meen
interesting مثير للاهتمام mutheer lil-ihtimaam
international دولي doowalee
International Student Card بطاقة طالب دولية biTaaqa Taalib doowaleeya
internet إنترنت internet
internet cafe مقهى إنترنت maqha internet
interpreter مترجم mutarjim
intersection ملتقى الطرق multaqee aT-Turuq
intestine أمعاء am'aa'
introduce يقدم yuqaddim
invoice n محاسبة muHaasaba
Iran إيران eeraan
Iranian إيراني eeraanee
Iraq العراق al-'iraaq
Iraqi عراقي 'iraaqee
Ireland أيرلندا eerlandaa
Irish أيرلندي eerlandee
iron (for clothes) مكواة mikwa
Israel إسرائيل israa'eel

**J**

jacket جاكيت jaakeet
jar مرطبان marTabaan
jaw فك fakk
jazz موسيقى الجاز mooseeqa al-jaaz
jazz club نادي لموسيقى الجاز naadee li-mooseeqa al-jaaz
jeans بنطلون جينز banTaloon jeenz
jet ski جت سكي jet-ski
jeweler محل المجوهرات maHal al-mujawharaat
jewelry مجوهرات mujawharaat

**joint (of body)** مفصل mifSal
**Jordan** الأردن al-urdun
**Jordanian** أردني urdunee

### K

**key** مفتاح miftaaH
**key card** كرت المفتاح kart al-miftaaH
**key ring** حمالة مفاتيح Hamaalat mafaateeH
**kiddie pool** مسبح للأطفال masbaH lil-aTfaal
**kidney (in body)** كلية kulya
**kilo** كيلو kilo
**kilogram** كيلوغرام kilogram
**kilometer** كيلومتر kilometer
**kiss** v يبوس yaboos
**kitchen** مطبخ maTbakh
**kitchen foil [BE]** رقائق المنيوم raqaa'iq aluminyoom
**knee** ركبة rukba
**knife** سكين sikeen
**Kuwait** الكويت al-kuwayt
**Kuwaiti** كويتي kuwaytee

### L

**lace** تخريم takhreem
**lactose intolerant** يتحسس من اللاكتوز yataHasas min al-laaktooz
**lake** بحيرة buHayra
**large** كبير kabeer
**last** آخر aakhar
**late (time)** متأخر muta'akhir
**launderette [BE]** محل تنظيف ألبسة بخدمة ذاتية maHal tanZeef albisa bi-khidma dhaateeya
**laundromat** محل تنظيف ألبسة بخدمة ذاتية maHal tanZeef albisa bi-khidma dhaateeya
**laundry** ملابس للغسيل malaabis lil-ghaseel
**laundry facility** مغسلة maghsala
**laundry service** خدمة غسيل ملابس khidma ghaseel malaabis
**lawyer** محامي muHaamee
**leather** جلد jild
**leave** v (deposit) يترك yatruk; (go away) يغادر yughaadir; (airplane) تغادر tughaadir
**Lebanese** لبناني lubnaanee
**Lebanon** لبنان lubnaan
**left (direction)** يسار yasaar
**leg** ساق saaq
**lens** عدسة 'adasa

**less** أقل aqal
**lesson** درس dars
**letter** رسالة risaala
**library** مكتبة maktaba
**Libya** ليبيا leebeeyaa
**Libyan** ليبي leebee
**life boat** قارب النجاة qaarib an-najaa
**lifeguard** منقذ munqidh
**life jacket** سترة النجاة sitrat an-najaa
**lift [BE]** مصعد miS'ad
**light** فاتح faatiH; n ضوء Daw'; v (cigarette) يشعل yash'al
**lightbulb** لمبة lamba
**lighter** ولاعة walaa'a
**like** v يحب yuHibb
**line** خط khaT
**linen** كتان kataan
**lip** شفة shiffa
**liquor store** محل المشروبات الكحولية maHal al-mashroobaat al-kuHooleeya
**liter** ليتر liter
**little** صغير Sagheer
**live** v يعيش ya'eesh
**live music** موسيقى حية mooseeqa Haya
**liver (in body)** كبد kabd
**loafers** موكاسان mookasaan
**local** محلي maHalee
**lock** n قفل qifl
**lock up** يقفل yaqful
**locker** خزانة khazaana
**log off** يخرج من الإنترنت yakhruj min al-internet
**log on** يدخل على الإنترنت yadkhul 'ala al-internet
**login** دخول dukhool
**long** طويل Taweel
**long-sighted [BE]** مصاب بمد النظر muSaab bi-madd an-naZar
**look** v يشوف yashoof
**loose (fit)** واسع waasi'
**lose (something)** يفقد yafqud
**lost** تائه taa'ih
**lost and found** الأمتعة المفقودة al-amti'at al-mafqooda
**lost property [BE]** الأمتعة المفقودة al-amti'at al-mafqooda
**lotion** غسول ghasool
**love** n محبة maHabba; v (someone) يحب yuHibb
**low** منخفض munkhafiD

low blood pressure ضغط دم منخفض DaghuT damm munkhafiD

luggage أمتعة amti'a

luggage cart عربات الأمتعة arabaat al-amti'a

luggage locker خزائن الأمتعة khazaa'in al-amti'a

luggage trolley [BE] عربات الأمتعة 'arabaat al-amti'a

lunch غذاء ghadhaa'

lung رئة ri'a

luxury car سيارة فخمة sayaara fakhma

## M

magazine مجلة majalla

magnificent جميل جداً jameel jiddan

mail n بريد bareed

mailbox صندوق البريد Sundooq al-bareed

mall مركز تجاري markaz tijaaree

man رجل rajul

manager مدير mudeer

manicure منيكور maneekoor

manual (car) بغيار عادي bi-ghiyar 'aadee

map خريطة khareeTa

market سوق sooq

married متزوج mutazawwij

mass (in church) قداس qudaas

massage مساج masaaj

match (game) لعبة lu'ba

matches كبريت kibreet

meal وجبة wajba

mean v يعني ya'nee

measuring cup فنجان للعيار finjaan lil-'ayaar

measuring spoon ملعقة للعيار mil'aqa lil-'ayaar

mechanic ميكانيكي meekaaneekee

medication دواء dawaa'

medicine دواء dawaa'

medium (size) متوسط mutawassiT

meet v يلتقي yaltaqee

meeting اجتماع ijtimaa'

meeting room قاعة اجتماعات qaa'at ijtimaa'aat

membership card بطاقة عضوية biTaaqa 'uDweeya

memory card كرت ذاكرة kart dhaakira

mend [BE] يصلح yuSalliH

menu قائمة الطعام qaa'imat aT-Ta'aam

menu of the day طبق اليوم Tabaq al-yawm

merge يدخل في السير yadkhul fee is-sayr

message رسالة risaala

microwave مايكروويف meekrooweyf

microwaveable مناسب للمايكروويف munaasib lil-meekroowayif

midday [BE] منتصف النهار muntaSif an-nahaar

midnight منتصف الليل muntaSif al-layl

mileage المسافة المقطوعة al-masaafat al-maqToo'a

mini-bar ميني بار meenee baar

minimum age أدنى adna

minute دقيقة daqeeqa

missing مفقود mafqood

mistake خطأ khaTaa'

mobile home بيت متنقل bayt mutanaqqal

mobile phone [BE] هاتف نقال haatif naqaal

moment لحظة laHZa

money مال maal

month شهر shahr

mop ممسحة mimsaHa

moped دراجة بمحرك daraaja bi-muHarrik

more أكثر akthar

morning صباح SabaaH

Moroccan مغربي maghrabee

Morocco المغرب al-maghrib

mosque جامع jaami'

mother أم umm

motion sickness دوار السفر dawaar as-safar

motorboat زورق zawraq

motorcycle دراجة نارية daraaja naareeya

motorway [BE] الطريق السريع aT-Tareeq as-saree'

mountain جبل jabal

mountain bike دراجة جبلية daraaja jabaleeya

mousse (hair) موس moos

mouth فم famm

movie فيلم feelm

movie theater صالة سينما Saala seenimaa

mugging سلب salb

muscle عضلة 'aDla

museum متحف matHaf

music موسيقى mooseeqa

music store محل سيديات maHal al-mooseeqa

Muslim مسلم muslim

## N

nail file مبرد للأظافر mibrad lil-aZaafir

nail salon صالون تجميل Saloon tajmeel

name اسم ism

napkin منديل للمائدة mandeel lil-maa'ida

nappy [BE] حفاضات HifaaDaat

**nationality** جنسية jinseeya
**nature preserve** محمية طبيعية maHmeeya Tabeeeeya
**nauseous** يشعر بغثيان yash'ur bi-ghathayaan
**near** قريب qareeb
**near-sighted** مصاب بقصر النظر muSaab bi-qaSr an-naZar
**neck** رقبة ruqba
**necklace** عقد 'uqd
**newspaper** جريدة jareeda
**next** تالي taalee
**nice** جميل jameel
**night** مساء masaa
**nightclub** نادي ليلي naadee laylee
**no** لا la
**non-alcoholic** بدون كحول bi-dooni kuHool
**non-smoking** لغير المدخنين li-ghayr al-mudakhineen
**noon** منتصف النهار muntaSif an-nahaar
**north** شمال shimaal
**nose** أنف anf
**not** ليس laysa
**nothing** لا شيء la shay
**notify** يخبر yukhbir
**now** الآن al-aan
**number** رقم raqm
**nurse** ممرض mumarriD

## O

**off (light, TV etc)** إيقاف eeqaaf
**office** مكتب maktab
**office hours** أوقات العمل awqaat al-'amal
**off-licence [BE]** محل المشروبات الكحولية maHal al-mashroobaat al-kuHooleeya
**oil** زيت zayt
**OK** حسناً Hasanan
**old** قديم qadeem
**old town** المدينة القديمة al-madeenat al-qadeema
**Oman** عمان omaan
**Omani** عماني omaanee
**on (light, TV etc)** تشغيل tashgheel
**once** مرة marra
**one** واحد waaHid
**one-way** ذهاب dhihaab
**only** فقط faqaT
**open** v يفتح yaftaH; adj مفتوح maftooH
**opposite** مقابل muqaabil
**optician** محل نظارات maHal naZaaraat

**orange (color)** برتقالي burtuqaalee
**orchestra** أوركسترا oorkistraa
**order** v يطلب yaTlub
**outdoor pool** مسبح masbaH
**outside** في الخارج fee il-khaarij
**overheated** ساخن أكثر من اللازم saakhin akthar min al-laazim
**overlook (scenic place)** إطلالة iTlaala
**overnight** طوال الليل Tawaal al-layl
**oxygen treatment** علاج بالأوكسجين 'ilaaj bil-awksijeen

## P

**p.m.** بعد الظهر ba'd aZ-Zuhr
**pacifier** لهاية lahaaya
**package** صندوق Sundooq
**paddling pool [BE]** مسبح أطفال masbaH aTfaal
**pain** ألم alam
**pajamas** بيجامة beejaama
**palace** قصر qaSr
**Palestine** فلسطين filisTeen
**Palestinian** فلسطيني filisTeenee
**pants** بنطلون banTaloon
**pantyhose** كولون kooloon
**paper** ورق waraq
**paper towel** مناشف ورقية manaashif warqeeya
**paracetamol [BE]** سيتامول seetaamool
**park** n حديقة عامة Hadeeqat 'aama; v (car) يصف yaSaff
**parking** موقف mawqif
**parking garage** موقف جراج mawqif garaaj
**parking lot** موقف سيارات mawqif sayaaraat
**parking meter** عداد الموقف 'adaad al-mawqif
**part (for car)** جزء juz'
**part-time** دوام جزئي dawaam juz'ee
**passenger** مسافر musaafir
**passport** جواز سفر jawaaz safar
**passport control** مراقبة جوازات السفر muraaqaba jawaazaat as-safar
**password** كلمة مرور kalima muroor
**pastry shop** محل حلويات maHal Hilweeyaat
**patch** يرقع yuraqi'
**path** ممر mamar
**pay** v يدفع yadfa'
**pay phone** هاتف عام haatif 'aam
**peak** n قمة qimma
**pearl** لؤلؤ loo'loo'
**pedestrian crossing [BE]** عبور مشاة 'uboor mushaa

**pedestrian crosswalk** عبور مشاة 'uboor mushaa

**pediatrician** طبيب أطفال Tabeeb aTfaal

**pedicure** بديكور bideekoor

**pen** قلم qalam

**penicillin** بنسلين penicillin

**penis** عضو ذكري 'aDoo dhikree

**perfume** عطر 'uTr

**period (menstruation)** عادة شهرية 'aada shahreeya; **(of time)** مدة mudda

**petite** صغير جدا Sagheer jiddan

**petrol [BE]** بنزين benzeen

**petrol station [BE]** محطة البنزين maHaTat al-binzeen

**pewter** قصدير qaSdeer

**pharmacy** صيدلية Saydleeya

**phone** n تلفون tilifoon; v يتصل yattaSil

**phone call** اتصال هاتفي ittiSaal haatifee

**phone card** بطاقة تلفونية biTaaqa tilifooneeya

**phone number** رقم تلفون raqm tilifoon

**photocopy** نسخة nuskha

**photograph** صورة Soora

**picnic area** منطقة النزهات manTaqat an-nuz-haat

**piece** قطعة qiT'a

**Pill (contraceptive)** حبوب منع الحمل Huboob mana' al-Haml

**pillow** مخدة mikhadda

**PIN** الرقم السري ar-raqm as-sirree

**pink** زهري zahree

**plan** خطة khuTTa

**plane** طائرة Taa'ira

**plastic wrap** غلاف نايلون ghilaaf naayloon

**plate** صحن SaHn

**platform** رصيف raSeef; **(at station) [BE]** خط khaT

**platinum** بلاتين blaateen

**play** n **(in theater)** مسرحية masraHeeya; v يلعب yal'ab

**playground** ملعب mal'ab

**playpen** مكان محاط بالشباك للعب makaan muHaaT bish-shubaak lil-la'ab

**please** من فضلك min faDlak

**plunger** غاطس ghaaTis

**point** v يشير yusheer

**poison** سم sam

**police** الشرطة ash-shurTa

**police report** تقرير الشرطة taqreer ash-shurTa

**police station** مركز الشرطة markaz ash-shurTa

**pond** بركة baraka

**pool** مسبح masbaH

**pop music** موسيقى البوب mooseeqa al-pop

**post [BE]** بريد bareed

**postbox [BE]** صندوق البريد Sundooq al-bareed

**postcard** كرت بوستال kart boostaal

**post office** البريد al-bareed

**pot** وعاء للطبخ wi'aa liT-Tabkh

**pottery** إناء فخاري inaa' fakhaaree

**pound (weight)** رطل raTl; **(sterling)** جنيه استرليني gunay istirleenee

**pregnant** حامل Haamil

**prepaid** مسبق الدفع musabaq ad-dafa'

**prescription** وصفة طبية waSfa Tibeeya

**press (clothes)** يكبس yikbis

**price** سعر si'r

**print** v يطبع yaTba'

**problem** مشكلة mushkila

**produce store** محل الخضار maHal al-khuDaar

**pull** v يسحب yis-Hab

**purple** بنفسجي banafsajee

**purse** حقيبة يد Haqeeba yad

**push** v يدفع yadfa'

**pushchair [BE]** عربة أطفال 'arabat aTfaal

**pyjamas [BE]** بيجامة beejaama

**Q**

**Qatar** قطر qaTar

**Qatari** قطري qaTaree

**quality** نوعية naw'eeya

**question** سؤال su'aal

**quiet** هادئ haadi'

**R**

**racetrack** مضمار السباق miDmaar as-sibaaq

**racket (sports)** مضرب miDrab

**railway station [BE]** محطة القطار maHaTat al-qiTaar

**rain** n مطر maTar

**raincoat** معطف للمطر mi'Taf lil-maTar

**rainy** ممطر mumTir

**rap (music)** موسيقى الراب mooseeqa ar-rap

**rape** n اغتصاب ightiSaab

**rash** n طفح جلدي TafH jildee

**razor** موس الحلاقة moos al-Hilaaqa

**razor blade** شفرات الحلاقة shafaraat al-Hilaaqa

**reach (person)** يجد yajid

**ready** جاهز jaahiz

real أصلي aSlee
receipt إيصال eeSaal
receive v يستقبل yastaqbil
reception استقبال istiqbaal
recharge v يشحن yash-Han
recommend ينصح yanSaH
recycling إعادة التصنيع i'aadat at-taSnee'
red أحمر aHmar
refrigerator ثلاجة thallaaja
refund n استرداد النقود istidaad an-nuqood
region منطقة manTaqa
regular عادي 'aadee
relationship (personal) علاقة 'ilaaqa
rent v يستأجر yasta'jir
rental car سيارة مستأجرة sayaara musta'jara
repair v يصلح yuSalliH
report v يبلغ عن yuballigh 'an
reservation حجز Hajz
reserve v يحجز yaHjuz
restaurant مطعم maT'am
restroom توواليت toowaaleet
retired متقاعد mutaqaa'id
return v يعود ya'ood; n [BE] ذهاب وعودة dhihaab wa-'awda
rib ضلع Dala'
right (correct) صحيح SaHeeH; (direction) يمين yameen
right of way أحقية الطريق aHqeeyat aT-Tareeq
ring n خاتم khaatim
river نهر nahr
road طريق Tareeq
road map خريطة طرق khareeTa Turuq
romantic رومانسي roomaansee
room غرفة ghurfa
room key مفتاح الغرفة miftaaH al-ghurfa
room service خدمة غرف khidma ghuruf
rotary دوار dawaar
round (in game) جولة jawla
roundabout [BE] دوار dawaar
round-trip ذهاب وعودة dhihaab wa-'awda
round-trip ticket تذكرة ذهاب و عودة tadhkara dhihaab wa-'awda
route طريق Tareeq
rubbish [BE] قمامة qamaama
rubbish bag [BE] أكياس قمامة akyaas qamaama
ruins آثار aathaar

**S**

sad حزين Hazeen
safe n خزينة khazeena; (not dangerous) آمن aamin; (not in danger) بأمان bi-amaan
sales tax ضريبة Dareeba
salty مالح maaliH
same نفس nafs
sandals صندل Sandal
sanitary napkin فوط نسائية fuwaT nisaa'eeya
sanitary pad [BE] فوط نسائية fuwaT nisaa'eeya
Saudi سعودي sa'oodee
Saudi Arabia السعودية as-sa'oodeeya
sauna ساونا saawnaa
save حفظ HafZ
savings account حساب المدخرات Hisaab al-mudkharaat
scanner ماسحة maasiHa
scarf لفاح lifaaH
schedule n جدول مواعيد jadwal mawaa'eed
school مدرسة madrassa
scissors مقص miqaSS
sea بحر baHr
seat مقعد maq'ad
security أمن aman
see يشوف yashoof
sell يبيع yabee'
self-service خدمة ذاتية khidma dhaateeya
seminar ندوة nadwa
send يرسل yursil
senior citizen مسنين musneen
separate منفصل munfaSil
serious خطير khaTeer
service خدمة khidma; (in church) صلاة Salaat
shampoo شامبو shaamboo
shaving cream كريم للحلاقة kreem lil-Hilaaqa
sheet شراشف sharaashif
shirt قميص qameeS
shoe store محل الأحذية maHal al-aHdheeya
shoes أحذية aHdheeya
shopping تسوق tasawooq
shopping area منطقة التسوق manTaqat at-tasawooq
shopping centre [BE] سوق تجاري markaz at-tijaaree
shopping mall سوق تجاري markaz at-tijaaree
short قصير qaSeer
shorts شورت shoort
short-sighted [BE] مصاب بقصر النظر muSaab

bi-qaSr an-naZar

**shoulder** كتف katif

**show** v يري yuree

**shower** دُش doosh

**shrine** مزار mazaar

**sick** مريض mareeD

**sightseeing tour** جولة لزيارة المعالم jawla li-ziyaarat al-ma'aalim

**sign** v يوقّع yuwaqi'a

**silk** حرير Hareer

**silver** فضة fiDDa

**single** عازب 'aazib

**single bed** سرير مفرد sareer mufrad

**single room** غرفة مفردة ghurfa mufrada

**single ticket [BE]** تذكرة ذهاب tadhkara dhihaab

**sister** أخت ukht

**sit** يجلس yajlis

**size** قياس qeeyaas

**skin** جلد jild

**skirt** تنورة tanoora

**sleeping bag** حقيبة للنوم Haqeeba lin-nawm

**slice** شريحة shareeHa

**slippers** شبشب shibshib

**slow** بطيء baTee'

**slowly** ببطء bi-buT'

**small** صغير Sagheer

**smoking** للمدخنين lil-mudakhineen

**snack bar** مطعم للوجبات الخفيفة maT'am lil-wajabaat al-khafeefa

**sneakers** أحذية رياضية aHdheeya reeyaaDeeya

**snorkeling equipment** شنركل snorkel

**snowy** يتساقط الثلج yatasaaqaT ath-thalj

**soap** صابون Saaboon

**soccer** كرة القدم kurrat al-qadam

**socks** جرابات juraabaat

**sold out** خلصت التذاكر khalaSat at-tadhaakir

**sore throat** ألم الحلق alam al-Halq

**sorry (apology)** آسف aasif

**south** جنوب janoob

**souvenir** هدايا تذكارية hadaayaa tidhkaareeya

**souvenir store** محل الهدايا التذكارية maHal al-hadaayaa at-tidhkaareeya

**spa** سبا spa

**sparkling water** مياه غازية miyaah ghaazeeya

**spatula** ملعقة مسطحة mil'aqa musaTaHa

**speak** يتكلم yatakallam

**special** خاص khaaS

**specialist** n أخصائي akhSaa'ee

**spicy** حار Haar

**spine** عمود فقري 'amood faqree

**spoon** ملعقة mil'aqa

**sporting goods store** محل الأدوات الرياضية maHal al-adawaat ar-reeyaaDeeya

**sprain** n التواء في المفصل iltiwaa' fee il-mifSal

**sprained** ملتوي multawee

**stadium** ملعب mal'ab

**stairs** دَرَج daraj

**stamp** n طابع Taabi'

**start** v يبدأ yabda'

**station** محطة maHaTat

**station wagon** سيارة بوكس sayaara books

**stay** v ينزل yanzil

**steal** يسرق yasriq

**steep** شديد الانحدار shadeed al-inHidaar

**sterling silver** فضة fiDDa

**stolen** مسروق masrooq

**stomach** معدة mi'da

**stomachache** ألم في المعدة alam fee il-mi'da

**stool (bowel movement)** براز biraaz

**stop** v يقف yaqif; n (on bus route) موقف mawqif

**store directory** دليل المحلات التجارية daleel al-maHalaat at-tijaareeya

**stove** فرن furn

**straight** مستقيم mustaqeem

**straight ahead** على طول 'ala Tool

**strange** غريب ghareeb

**stream** جدول jadwal

**street** شارع shaari'

**stroller** عربة أطفال 'arabat aTfaal

**student** طالب Taalib

**study** v يدرس yadrus

**stunning** مذهل mudh-hil

**subway** مترو الأنفاق metro al-anfaaq

**subway station** محطة مترو الأنفاق maHaTat metro al-anfaaq

**Sudan** السودان as-soodaan

**Sudanese** سوداني soodaanee

**suit (clothing)** طقم Taqm

**suitable** مناسب munaasib

**suitcase** حقيبة Haqeeba

**sun** شمس shams

**sunblock** واقي شمسي waaqee shamsee

sunburn حروق شمسية Hurooq shamseeya
sunglasses نظارات شمسية naZaaraat shamseeya
sunny مشمس mushmis
sunscreen واقي شمسي waaqee shamsee
sunstroke ضربة شمس Darba shams
super (fuel) ممتاز mumtaaz
supermarket سوبر ماركت soobir maarkit
surcharge أجرة إضافية ujrat iDaafeeya
surfboard لوح لركوب الأمواج looH li-rukoob al-amwaaj
surgical spirit [BE] كحول طبي kuHool Tibbee
swallow v يبتلع yabtala'
sweater كنزة صوف kanza Soof
sweatshirt كنزة رياضة kanza reeyaaDa
sweet حلو Hiloo
sweets [BE] سكاكر sakaakir
swim v يسبح yasbaH
swimsuit مايوه maayooh
Syria سوريا sooriyaa
Syrian سوري sooree

## T

table طاولة Taawila
tablet حبة Habba
take v يأخذ ya'khudh
take off (shoes) يخلع yikhla'
tampon سدادات قطنية للسيدات sadadaat quTneeya lis-sayyidaat
taste v يتذوق yatadhawwaq
taxi تاكسي taaksee
tea شاي shaay
team فريق fareeq
teaspoon ملعقة صغيرة mil'aqa Sagheera
telephone تلفون tilifoon
temple (religious) معبد ma'bad
temporary مؤقت mu'aqat
tennis التنس at-tinnis
tennis court ملاعب تنس malaa'ib tinnis
tent خيمة khayma
tent peg أوتاد الخيمة awtaad al-khayma
tent pole عمود الخيمة amood al-khayma
terminal (airport) تيرمينال teerminaal
terrible فظيع faZee'
text v يبعث اس ام اس yab'ath SMS; n اس ام اس SMS
thank you! شكراً shukran
that ذلك dhaalik
theater مسرح masraH

theft سرقة sirqa
there هناك hunaak
thief لص liSS
thigh فخذ fakhdh
thirsty عطشان 'aTshaan
this هذا haadha
throat حلق Halq
thunderstorm عاصفة رعدية 'aaSifa ra'deeya
ticket تذكرة tadhkara
ticket office مكتب التذاكر maktab at-tadhaakir
tie n كرافت kraafeet
tight (fit) ضيق Dayyiq
tights [BE] كولون kooloon
time وقت waqt
timetable [BE] جدول مواعيد jadwal mawaa'eed
tire دولاب doolaab
tired تعبان ta'baan
tissue مناديل ورقية manaadeel warqeeya
to إلى ila
today اليوم al-yawm
toe إصبع القدم iSba' al-qadam
toenail ظفر إصبع القدم Zifr iSba' al-qadam
toilet [BE] تواليت toowaaleet
toilet paper ورق تواليت waraq toowaaleet
toll road طريق برسم مرور Tareeq bi-rasm muroor
tomorrow غد ghadan
tonight الليلة al-layla
too (also) أيضاً ayDaan; (excessively) أكثر من اللازم akthar min al-laazim
tooth سن sinn
toothache ألم في الأسنان alam fee il-asnaan
toothbrush فرشاة أسنان furshaat asnaan
toothpaste معجون أسنان ma'joon asnaan
torch [BE] بيل beel
total (amount) مجمل mujmal
tour جولة jawla
tourist سائح saa'iH
tourist information office مكتب الاستعلامات السياحية maktab al-isti'laamaat as-seeyaaHeeya
tow truck شاحنة قاطرة shaaHina qaaTira
towel منشفة minshafa
tower برج burj
town مدينة madeena
town hall البلدية al-baladeeya
town map خريطة المدينة khareeTat al-madeena
town square ساحة المدينة saaHat al-madeena

**toy** لعبة أطفال lu'bat aTfaal
**toy store** محل ألعاب الأطفال maHal al'aab al-aTfaal
**track (for trains)** خط khaT
**traditional** تقليدي taqleedee
**traffic circle** دوار dawaar
**traffic light** إشارة مرور ishaarat muroor
**trail** ممر mamar
**trailer** عربة مقطورة 'araba maqToora
**train** n قطار qiTaar
**train station** محطة قطار maHaTat qiTaar
**transfer v (traveling)** يبدل yubaddil
**translate** يترجم yutarjim
**trash** قمامة qamaama
**travel agency** مكتب سياحة و سفر maktab seeyaaHa wa safar
**travelers check** شيك سياحي sheek seeyaaHee
**traveller's cheque [BE]** شيك سياحي sheek seeyaaHee
**travel sickness** دوار السفر dawaar as-safar
**tree** شجرة shajara
**trim (haircut)** تطريف شعر taTreef sha'r
**trip** رحلة riHla
**trolley [BE]** عربة 'araba
**trousers [BE]** بنطلون banTaloon
**T-shirt** تي شيرت tee sheert
**tumble dry** يعصر في الغسالة yu'aSar fee il-ghasaala
**Tunisia** تونس toonis
**Tunisian** تونسي toonisee
**turn off (light)** يطفئ yaTfa'
**turn on (light)** يشعل yash'al
**TV** تلفزيون tilifizyoon
**tyre [BE]** دولاب doolaab

**U**

**ugly** بشع bashi'
**umbrella** مظلة maZalla
**underground [BE]** مترو الأنفاق metro al-anfaaq
**underground station [BE]** محطة مترو الأنفاق maHaTat metro al-anfaaq
**underpants [BE]** سروال داخلي sirwaal daakhilee
**understand** يفهم yafham
**underwear** ملابس داخلية malaabis dakhileeya
**United Kingdom** بريطانيا breeTaaneeyaa
**United States** أمريكا amreekaa
**unleaded** بدون رصاص bi-dooni raSaaS
**unlimited mileage** بأميال غير محدودة bi-amyaal ghayr maHdooda

**urgent** مستعجل musta'jil
**urine** بول bool
**use** v يستخدم yastakhdim
**username** اسم المستخدم ism al-mustakhdim
**utensil** أدوات الطبخ adawaat aT-Tabkh

**V**

**vacation** إجازة ijaaza
**vacuum cleaner** مكنسة كهربائية miknasa kahrabaa'eeya
**vagina** مهبل mahbil
**vaginal infection** التهاب مهبلي iltihaab mahbilee
**valley** وادي waadee
**value** n قيمة qeema
**van** فان van
**VAT [BE]** ضريبة Dareeba
**vegan** لا يأكل المنتجات الحيوانية la ya'kul al-muntajaat al-Haywaaneeya
**vegetarian** نباتي nabaatee
**vehicle registration** تسجيل سيارة tasjeel sayaara
**vending machine** ماكينة بيع maakeena bay'
**very** جداً jiddan
**viewpoint [BE]** إطلالة iTlaala
**visit** v يزور yazoor
**visiting hours** مواعيد الزيارة mawaa'eed az-ziyaara
**visually impaired** نظره ضعيف naZarhu Da'eef
**volleyball** كرة الطائرة kurrat aT-Taa'ira
**vomiting** يتقيأ yataqayaa'

**W**

**wait** v ينتظر yantaZar
**waiter** غرسون gharsoon
**waiting room** غرفة انتظار ghurfat intiZaar
**waitress** آنسة aanisa
**wake (person)** يوقظ yawqiZ
**wake-up call** مكالمة إيقاظ mukaalamat eeqaaZ
**walk** n نزهة nuz-ha
**walking route** طرق السير Turuq as-sayr
**wallet** محفظة miHfaZa
**warm** دافئ daafi'; v يسخن yusakhin
**wash** v يغسل yughassal
**washing machine** غسالة الملابس ghasaalat al-malaabis
**washing-up liquid [BE]** سائل للجلي saa'il lil-jallee
**watch** n ساعة يد saa'a yad
**water** ماء maa'

**waterfall** شلال shalaal
**water skis** ألواح للتزحلق على الماء al-waaH lit-tazaHluq ʿala al-maaʾ
**weather** طقس Taqs
**week** أسبوع usbooʿ
**weekend** عطلة نهاية الأسبوع ʿuTla nihaayat al-usbooʿ
**weekly** أسبوعي usbooʿee
**well-rested** مرتاح murtaaH
**west** غرب gharb
**what** ماذا maadha
**wheelchair** كرسي المقعدين kursee al-muqʿadeen
**wheelchair ramp** منحدر خاص لكرسي المقعدين munHadir khaaS li-kursee al-muqʿadeen
**when** متى mata
**where** أين ayn
**where to** إلى أين ila ayn
**which** أي ay
**white** أبيض abyaD
**white gold** ذهب أبيض dhahab abyaD
**who** من man
**widowed** أرمل armal
**wife** زوجة zawja
**window** نافذة naafidha
**window seat** مقعد على النافذة maqʿad ʿala an-naafidha
**windsurfer** لوح شراعي looH shiraaʿee
**wine list** قائمة النبيذ qaaʾimat an-nabeedh
**wireless internet** إنترنت لاسلكي internet lasilkee

**wireless internet service** خدمة إنترنت لاسلكي khidmat internet lasilkee
**with** مع maʿ
**withdraw** يسحب yas-Hab
**without** بدون bi-doon
**woman** امرأة imraaʾa
**wool** صوف Soof
**work** v يعمل yaʿmal
**wrist** معصم miʿSam
**write (down)** يكتب yuktub

**Y**

**year** سنة sana
**yellow** أصفر aSfar
**yellow gold** ذهب أصفر dhahab aSfar
**Yemen** اليمن al-yaman
**Yemeni** يمني yamanee
**yes** نعم naʿam
**yesterday** البارحة al-baariHa
**yield (in traffic)** أعط أحقية الطريق aʿaT aHaqeeyat aT-Tareeq
**yogurt** لبن laban
**young** شاب shaab
**you're welcome** عفواً ʿafwaan
**youth hostel** بيت شباب bayt shabaab

**Z**

**zoo** حديقة الحيوانات Hadeeqat al-Hayawaanaat

---

**A**

**aʿaT aHaqeeyat aT-Tareeq** أعط أحقية الطريق yield [give way BE]
**aʿmaal** أعمال business
**ʿaada shahreeya** عادة شهرية period (menstruation)
**ʿaadee** عادي regular
**ʿaaʾila** عائلة family
**aakhar** آخر another
**aakhir** آخر last
**ʿaalee** عالي high
**aamin** آمن safe (not dangerous)
**aanisa** آنسة waitress

**aasif** آسف sorry
**ʿaaSifa raʿdeeya** عاصفة رعدية thunderstorm
**aathaar** آثار ruin
**aathaar jaanibeeya** آثار جانبية side effect
**ʿaazib** عازب single
**ab** أب father
**abyaD** أبيض white
**ʿadaad al-mawqif** عداد الموقف parking meter
**ʿadasa** عدسة lens
**ʿadasa laaSiqa** عدسة لاصقة contact lens
**adawaat aT-Tabkh** أدوات الطبخ utensil
**ʿadeem an-nuk-ha** عديم النكهة bland (food)

adna 'umr أدنى عمر minimum age
'aDla عضلة muscle
'aDu dhikree عضو ذكري penis
afDal أفضل better
'afwaan عفواً that's ok
aHaqeeyat aT-Tareeq أحقية الطريق right of way
aHdheeya أحذية shoes
aHdheeya reeyaaDeeya أحذية رياضية sneakers
ahlaan wa sahlaan أهلاً و سهلاً you're welcome
aHmar أحمر red
aHsan أحسن best
AIDS أيدز aydz
akh أخ brother
akhDar أخضر green
akhSaa'ee أخصائي specialist n
akthar أكثر more
akthar min al-laazim أكثر من اللازم excessively, too
akyaas qamaama أكياس قمامة garbage bag [bin bag BE]
'ala Tool على طول straight ahead
al-aan الآن now
alam ألم pain
alam al-Halq ألم الحلق sore throat
alam fee il-asnaan ألم في الأسنان toothache
alam fee il-mi'da ألم في المعدة stomach ache
alam fee iS-Sadr ألم في الصدر chest pain
alam fee il-udhn ألم في الأذن earache
alam fee iZ-Zuhr ألم في الظهر backache
al-amti'a al-mafqooda الأمتعة المفقودة lost and found [lost property BE]
'alaykum عليكم hello
al-baariHa البارحة yesterday
alghee الغي cancel
al-khaleej al-'arabee الخليج العربي Gulf (Persian)
al-layla الليلة tonight
al-maas ألماس diamond
al-waaH lit-tazaHluq 'ala al-maa' ألواح للتزحلق على الماء water ski
al-wuSool الوصول arrivals (airport)
al-yawm اليوم today
aman أمن security
'amood faqree عمود فقري spine
'amood lil-khayma عمود الخيمة tent pole
amreekaa أمريكا United States
amreekaanee أمريكي American
amti'a أمتعة luggage

anf أنف nose
aqal أقل less
'araba عربة cart [trolley BE]
'araba maqToora عربة مقطورة trailer
'arabat al-amti'a عربات الأمتعة luggage cart [trolley BE]
'arabat aTfaal عربة أطفال stroller [pushchair BE]
'arabee عربي Arab, Arabic; al-'arabeeya العربية Arabic (language)
araq أرق insomnia
'arboon عربون deposit
arD أرض floor
arD al-golf أرض الغولف golf course
arD baalayh عرض باليه ballet
arD oobiraa عرض أوبرا opera
armal أرمل widowed
aSam أصم deaf
asbireen أسبرين aspirin
'aSeer عصير juice
aSfar أصفر yellow
'ashaa عشاء dinner
aSlee أصلي real
aswad أسود black
'aTshaan عطشان thirsty
awal أول first
awqaat al-'amal أوقات العمل office hours
awqaat al-'amal أوقات العمل business hours
awtaad al-khayma أوتاد الخيمة tent peg
awtoomaateekee أوتوماتيكي automatic
ay أي which
ay shay أي شيء anything
ayDan أيضاً too (also)
ayn أين where
'ayn عين eye
'aZm عظم bone
azraq أزرق blue

B

baab باب door
ba'ad بعد after
ba'ad aZ-Zuhr بعد الظهر afternoon, p.m.
baar بار bar
baarid بارد cold adj
baarid qaleelan بارد قليلاً cool (temperature)
baaS باص bus
baaS saree' باص سريع express bus

ba'eed بعيد far
baHr بحر sea
baHraynee بحريني Bahraini; al-baHrayn البحرين Bahrain
baladeeya البلدية town hall
balsam بلسم conditioner
banafsajee بنفسجي purple
bank بنك bank
banTaloon بنطلون pants [trousers BE]
banTaloon jeenz بنطلون جينز jeans
baraka بركة pond
bareed بريد mail n [post BE], post office
bareed iliktroonee بريد إلكتروني e-mail
baysbool بيسبول baseball
bashi' بشع ugly
baTaareeya بطارية battery
baTaneeya بطانية blanket
baTee' بطيء slow
bawaaba بوابة gate (at airport)
bawabaat as-safar بوابات السفر departure gate
bayj بيج beige
bayt بيت house
bayt mutanaqal بيت متنقل mobile home
bayt shabaab بيت شباب youth hostel
bideekoor بديكور pedicure
beejaama بيجامة pajamas [pyjamas BE]
beel بيل flashlight [torch BE]
binzeen بنزين gas [petrol BE]
bi-amaan بأمان safe, not in danger
bi-buT' بيطء slowly
biDaa'i lil-i'laan 'anhaa بضائع للإعلان عنها goods to declare
biDaa'i mu'afeeya min aD-Daraa'ib بضائع معفية من الضرائب duty-free goods
bi-doon بدون without
bi-dooni raSaaS بدون رصاص unleaded
bi-ittijah markaz al-madeena باتجاه مركز المدينة downtown
bi-ghiyar 'aadee بغيار عادي manual (car)
bi-munfaridih بمفرده alone
penicillin (binisileen) بنسلين penicillin
bint بنت girl
biraaz براز stool (bowel movement)
biTaaqa بطاقة card
biTaaqa tilifooneeya بطاقة تلفونية phone card
biTaaqa 'uDweeya بطاقة عضوية membership card

biTaaqat i'timaan بطاقة ائتمان credit card
biTaaqat Su'ood بطاقة صعود boarding pass
biTaaqa Taalib doowaleeya بطاقة طالب دولية International Student Card
biTaaqa ta'meen بطاقة تأمين insurance card
blaateen بلاتين platinum
blooza بلوزة blouse
bool بول urine
breeTaanee بريطاني British adj
breeTaaneeyaa بريطانيا United Kingdom
broosh بروش brooch
buHayra بحيرة lake
bunnee بني brown
bunshur بنشر flat (on vehicle)
burj برج tower
burtuqaal برتقال orange (fruit)
burtuqaalee برتقالي orange (color)

## D

daafi' دافئ warm
daakhil داخل inside
Dala' ضلع rib
daleel دليل guide
daleel al-maHalaat at-tijaareeya دليل المحلات التجارية store directory
Damaadaat ضمادات bandage
damm دم blood
daqeeqa دقيقة minute
daraaja دراجة bicycle
daraaja bi-muHarik دراجة بمحرك moped
daraaja jabaleeya دراجة جبلية mountain bike
daraaja naareeya دراجة نارية motorcycle
daraj دَرَج stair
darajat oola درجة أولى first class
daraja seeyaaHeeya درجة سياحية economy class
darajaat درجات degrees (temperature)
darajat al-a'maal درجة الأعمال business class
Darbat shams ضربة شمس sunstroke
Dareeba ضريبة sales tax [VAT BE]
dars درس lesson
dawaa' دواء medication, medicine
dawaa' bidooni 'alaama tijaareeya دواء بدون علامة تجارية generic drug
dawaam juz'ee دوام جزئي part-time
dawaar دوار traffic circle [roundabout BE]
dawaar as-safar دوار السفر motion [travel BE] sickness

**daw'** ضوء light *n*
**Dayyiq** ضيق tight (fit)
**dee fee dee** دي في دي DVD
**deezil** ديزل diesel
**dhaalik** ذلك that
**dhahab** ذهب gold
**dhahab abyaD** ذهب أبيض white gold
**dhahab aSfar** ذهب أصفر yellow gold
**dhihaab** ذهاب one-way [single BE] (ticket)
**dhihaab wa-'awda** ذهاب وعودة round-trip [return *n* BE] (ticket)
**dhiraa'** ذراع arm
**dijeetaal** دجيتال digital
**doolaab** دولاب tire [tyre BE]
**doolaar** دولار dollar
**doosh** دُش shower
**doowalee** دولي international
**duf'a musabbaqa** دفعة مسبقة cash advance
**DaghuT damm munkhafiD** ضغط دم منخفض low blood pressure
**DaghuT damm murtafi'** ضغط دم مرتفع high blood pressure
**dukhool** دخول login
**dumya** دمية doll
**duzeena** دزينة dozen

## E

**'eed meelaad** عيد ميلاد birthday
**eedaa'** إيداع deposit (at bank)
**eeqaaf** إيقاف off
**eeraan** إيران Iran
**eeraanee** إيراني Iranian
**eerlandaa** أيرلندا Ireland
**eerlandee** أيرلندي Irish
**eeSaal** إيصال receipt

## F

**faarigh** فارغ empty *adj*
**faatiH** فاتح light
**faHam** فحم charcoal
**fakhdh** فخذ thigh
**fakk** فك jaw
**famm** فم mouth
**faqaT** فقط only
**faraama** فرامة food processor
**faraamil** فرامل brake

**fareeq** فريق team
**fataaHat an-nabeedh** فتاحة النبيذ corkscrew
**fataaHat zujaajaat** فتاحة زجاجات bottle opener
**faaks** فاكس fax
**faZee'** فظيع terrible
**fee** في in
**fee il-khaarij** في الخارج outside
**feelm** فيلم movie, film (camera)
**fee iS-SubH** في الصبح a.m.
**fiDDa** فضة silver
**filisTeen** فلسطين Palestine
**filisTeenee** فلسطيني Palestinian
**finjaan** فنجان cup
**finjaan lil-'ayaar** فنجان للعيار measuring cup
**fireezir** فريزر freezer
**fitreenaa** فترينا display case
**flaash** فلاش flashlight [torch BE]
**funduq** فندق hotel
**furn** فرن stove
**furn mukhayyam** فرن مخيم camping stove
**furshaat ash-sha'r** فرشاة الشعر hairbrush
**furshaat asnaan** فرشاة أسنان toothbrush
**fustaan** فستان dress (woman's)
**fuToor** فطور breakfast
**fuwaT nisaa'eeya** فوط نسائية sanitary napkins [sanitary pads BE]

## G

**garaaj** جراج garage
**ghaaba** غابة forest
**ghaalee** غالي expensive
**ghaamik** غامق dark
**ghaaz aT-Tabkh** غاز الطبخ cooking gas
**ghadan** غداً tomorrow
**ghadhaa'** غذاء lunch
**gharb** غرب west
**ghareeb** غريب strange
**gharsoon** غرسون waiter
**ghasaalat al-malaabis** غسالة الملابس washing machine
**ghasaalat aS-SuHoon** غسالة الصحون dishwasher
**ghasool** غسول lotion
**ghayr mashghool** غير مشغول available
**ghayr muklif** غير مكلف inexpensive
**gram (ghraam)** غرام gram
**ghurfa** غرفة room

**ghurfa fee iT-Taabiq al-arDee** غرفة في الطابق الأرضي ground-floor room

**ghurfa mufrada** غرفة مفردة single room

**ghurfa muzdawwaja** غرفة مزدوجة double room

**ghurfat intiZaar** غرفة انتظار waiting room

**ghurfa nawm** غرفة نوم dormitory

**ghurfa qeeyaas** غرفة قياس fitting room

**ghurfa Ta'aam** غرفة طعام dining room

**golf** الغولف golf

**gunay istirleenee** جنيه استرليني pound (sterling)

**H**

**haadi** هادئ quiet

**Haadith** حادث accident

**Haadith iSTidaam** حادث اصطدام crash n (in car)

**Haamil** حامل pregnant

**Haar** حار hot (spicy)

**haatif 'aam** هاتف عام pay phone

**haatif naqaal** هاتف نقال cell [mobile BE] phone

**haay laayt** هاي لايت highlights (in hair)

**Habba** حبة tablet

**hadaayaa tidhkaareeya** هدايا تذكارية souvenir

**Hadeeqa 'aama** حديقة عامة park n

**Hadeeqat al-Hayawanaat** حديقة الحيوانات zoo

**Hadeeqat an-nabaataat** حديقة النباتات botanical garden

**hadeeya** هدية gift

**Hafeed** حفيد grandchild

**Hafla mooseeqeeya** حفلة موسيقية concert

**HafZ** حفظ save

**Hajz** حجز reservation

**Halaal** حلال halal

**Halaaq rijaalee** حلاق رجالي barber

**Halaq** حلق earrings

**Halq** حلق throat

**Hamaalaat mafaateeH** حمالة مفاتيح key ring

**Hamaalaat Sadr** حمالة صدر bra

**Hamaam** حمام bathroom

**Haqeeba** حقيبة suitcase

**Haqeeba lin-nawm** حقيبة للنوم sleeping bag

**Haqeeba yad** حقيبة يد carry-on [hand luggage BE]

**Haqeeba yad** حقيبة يد purse [handbag BE]

**Haqeeba Zuhr** حقيبة ظهر backpack

**Haql** حقل field

**Haraara murtafi'a** حرارة مرتفعة fever

**Hareeq** حريق fire

**Hareer** حرير silk

**Harq** حرق burn n

**Hasanan** حسناً OK

**haSeera** حصيرة groundcloth [groundsheet BE]

**Hasharaat** حشرات bug

**Hashwa** حشوة filling (in tooth)

**haweeya shakhSeeya** هوية شخصية ID

**Haywaan** حيوان animal

**haadha** هذا this

**Hazeen** حزين sad

**Hiloo** حلو sweet

**Hizaam** حزام belt

**HifaaDaat** حفاضات diaper [nappy BE]

**Hisaab** حساب account; bill; check (in restaurant)

**Hisaab al-jaaree** حساب الجاري checking account

**Hisaab al-mudakharaat** حساب المدخرات savings account

**HiSn** حصن fort

**Huboob mana' al-Haml** حبوب منع الحمل Pill (contraceptive)

**Hummi il-qash** حمى القش hay fever

**huna** هنا here

**hunaak** هناك there

**Hurayraat** حريرات calorie

**Hurooq shamseeya** حروق شمسية sunburn

**Hurr** حر heat

**I**

**i'aadat at-taSnee'** إعادة التصنيع recycling

**i'tidaa'** اعتداء attack

**i'timaan** ائتمان credit

**ibreeq** إبريق carafe

**iDaafee** إضافي extra

**ightiSaab** اغتصاب rape n

**iHtiqaan** احتقان congestion

**ijaaza** إجازة vacation [holiday BE]

**ijra'aat as-safar** إجراءات السفر check-in

**ijra'aat as-safar lit-tadhaakir al-iliktrooneeya** إجراءات السفر للتذاكر الالكترونية e-ticket check-in

**ijtimaa'** اجتماع meeting

**ila** إلى to

**ila ayn** إلى أين where to

**'ilaaj aroomaatee** علاج أروماتي aromatherapy

**'ilaaj bil-ibar** علاج بالإبر acupuncture

**'ilaaj bil-awksijeen** علاج بالأوكسجين oxygen treatment

**'ilaaqa** علاقة relationship (personal)

'ilka علكة chewing gum
iltihaab mafaaSil التهاب مفاصل arthritis
iltihaab mahbalee التهاب مهبلي vaginal infection
iltiwaa' fee il-mifSal التواء في المفصل sprain n
im'aa أمعاء intestine
imraa'a امرأة woman
inaa' fakharee إناء فخاري pottery
ingleezee إنكليزي English; al-ingleezeeya الانكليزية English (language)
insooleen انسولين insulin
internet إنترنت internet
internet lasilkee إنترنت لاسلكي wireless internet
iqtiHaam اقتحام break-in
'iraaqee عراقي Iraqi; al-'iraaq العراق Iraq
iSba' إصبع finger
iSba' al-qadam إصبع القدم toe
is-haal إسهال diarrhea
ishaarat al-muroor إشارة المرور traffic light
ism اسم name
ism al-mustakhdim اسم المستخدم username
israa'eel إسرائيل Israel
isti'laamaat استعلامات information (telephone)
[directory enquiries BE], information desk
istilaam al-Haqaa'ib استلام الحقائب baggage claim
istiqbaal استقبال reception
istimaara استمارة form (to fill in)
istimaara muTaalaba استمارة مطالبة claim form
istirdaad an-nuqood استرداد النقود refund n
iTfaa' إطفاء fire department
itijaah اتجاه direction
iTalaala إطلالة overlook (scenic place) [viewpoint BE]
ittiSaal اتصال connection
ittiSaal haatifee اتصال هاتفي phone call

## J

jaa'i' جائع hungry
jaahiz جاهز ready
jaakeet جاكيت jacket
jaami' جامع mosque
jabal جبل mountain
jadd جد grandparent
jadwal جدول stream
jadwal mawaa'eed جدول مواعيد schedule [timetable BE]
jameel جميل beautiful, nice, cute
jameel jiddan جميل جداً magnificent

janoob جنوب south
jareeda جريدة newspaper
jawaaz safar جواز سفر passport
jayyid جيد fine, good
jadhaab جذاب attractive (person)
jazaa'iree جزائري Algerian; al-jazaa'ir الجزائر Algeria
jazma جزمة boot
jazma mareeHa lil-mashi جزمة مريحة للمشي hiking boot
jeenz جينز denim
jet-ski جت سكي jet ski
jiddan جداً very
jil جل gel
jild جلد leather, skin
jeemnaaziyoom جيمنازيوم gym
jinseeya جنسية nationality
jisr جسر bridge
jisr munkhafiD جسر منخفض low bridge
jawla جولة round (in game), tour
jawla bil-baaS جولة بالباص bus tour
jawla li-ziyaarat al-ma'aalim جولة لزيارة المعالم sightseeing tour
jumruk جمرك customs
juraabaat جرابات sock
jurH جرح cut n
juz' جزء part (for car)

## K

kaabeena كابينة cabin
kaaHil كاحل ankle
kaameeraa كاميرا camera
kaameeraa dijeetaal كاميرا ديجيتال digital camera
kaash كاش cash
kabd كبد liver (in body)
kabeer كبير big
kabeer jiddan كبير جداً extra large
kahf كهف cave
kalb irshaad al-'umyaan كلب إرشاد العميان guide dog
kalimat al-muroor كلمة مرور password
kam al-Hisaab كم الحساب how much
kanadaa كندا Canada
kanadee كندي Canadian
kaneesa كنيسة church
kanza reeyaaDa كنزة رياضة sweatshirt
kanza Soof كنزة صوف sweater
kart al-a'maal كرت الأعمال business card

**kart al-miftaH** كرت المفتاح key card
**kart boostaal** كرت بوستال postcard
**kart dhaakira** كرت ذاكرة memory card
**kartoona** كرتونة carton
**ka's** كأس glass (for drink)
**kataan** كتان linen
**katif** كتف shoulder
**kayf** كيف how
**kazeenoo** كازينو casino
**kees** كيس bag
**kees qamaama** كيس قمامة garbage bag [bin bag BE]
**khaal min ad-dasm** خال من الدسم fat free
**khaaS** خاص special
**khaaS lil-mu'aaqeen** خاص للمعاقين handicapped-accessible
**khaaTib** خاطب engaged
**khaatim** خاتم ring n
**khalaaT** خلاط blender
**khalaSat at-tadhaakir** خلصت التذاكر sold out
**khalf** خلف behind
**khareeTa** خريطة map
**khareeTat al-madeena** خريطة المدينة town map
**khareeTa Turuq** خريطة طرق road map
**khaT** خط line
**khaTaa'** خطأ mistake
**khaTeer** خطير dangerous, serious
**khaT** خط track (for train) [platform BE]
**khayma** خيمة tent
**khazaana** خزانة locker
**khazaf** خزف enamel
**khazeena** خزينة safe n
**khazaa'in al-amti'a** خزائن الأمتعة luggage locker
**khidma kaamila** خدمة كاملة full-service
**khidma dhateeya** خدمة ذاتية self-service
**khidmaat tanZeef** خدمات تنظيف housekeeping service
**khidma ghaseel malaabis** خدمة غسيل ملابس laundry service
**khidma ghuruf** خدمة غرف room service
**khidmat internet lasilkee** خدمة إنترنت لاسلكي wireless internet service
**khidma** خدمة service
**khilaal** خلال during
**khoodha** خوذة helmet
**khumool** خمول drowsiness
**khurooj** خروج exit

**khuTooT jaweeya** خطوط جوية airline
**khuTTa** خطة plan
**kibreet** كبريت matches
**kilo** كيلو kilo
**kilogram** كيلوغرام kilogram
**kilometer** كيلومتر kilometer
**kitaab** كتاب book
**kitaab 'an al-makaan** كتاب عن المكان guide book
**kooloon** كولون pantyhose [tights BE]
**kooloonyaa** كولونيا cologne
**koorn fliks** كورن فلكس cereal
**koowaafeer** كوافير hairstylist
**kraafeet** كرافيت tie n
**kreem lil-Hilaaqa** كريم للحلاقة shaving cream
**kreem mu'qim** كريم معقم antiseptic cream
**kreestaal** كريستال crystal
**kuHool Tibbee** كحول طبي rubbing alcohol [surgical spirit BE]
**kulfat al-mukaalamat 'ala al-muttaSil** كلفة المكالمة على المتصل call collect
**kulya** كلية kidney (in body)
**kumbyootir** كومبيوتر computer
**kurrat al-qadam** كرة القدم soccer [football BE]
**kurrat as-silla** كرة السلة basketball
**kurrat aT-Taa'ira** كرة الطائرة volleyball
**kursee** كرسي chair
**kursee 'aalin** كرسي عالي highchair
**kursee al-muq'adeen** كرسي المقعدين wheelchair
**kursee khaaS lil-aTfaal** كرسي خاص للأطفال child's seat
**kursee lish-shaaTee'** كرسي للشاطئ deck chair
**kuwaytee** كويتي Kuwaiti; **al-kuwayt** الكويت Kuwait

## L

**la** لا no
**la shay** لا شيء nothing
**laaHiqan** لاحقاً later
**ladghat al-Hasharaat** لدغة الحشرات insect bite
**ladheedh** لذيذ delicious
**laHaam** لحام butcher
**lahaaya** لهاية pacifier [dummy BE]
**laHZa** لحظة moment
**lamba** لمبة lightbulb
**lawaazim Tabkh** لوازم طبخ cooking facility
**laysa** ليس not
**leebee** ليبي Libyan

leebeeyaa ليبيا Libya
li- لـ for
libaas munaasib لباس مناسب dress code
lifaaH لفاح scarf
li-ghayr al-mudakhineen لغير المدخنين non-smoking
lil-isti'maal marra waaHida للاستعمال مرة واحدة disposable
lil-mudakhineen للمدخنين smoking
lisaan لسان tongue
liSS لص thief
liter لیتر liter
looH li-rukoob al-amwaaj لوح لركوب الأمواج surfboard
looH shiraa'ee لوح شراعي windsurfer
loo'loo' لؤلؤ pearl
lu'ba لعبة game
lu'ba لعبة match (game)
lu'bat aTfaal لعبة أطفال toy
lubnaan لبنان Lebanon
lubnaanee لبناني Lebanese

## M

ma' مع with
ma' as-salaama مع السلامة goodbye
maa ماء water
maa' saakhin ماء ساخن hot water
maadha ماذا what
ma'joon asnaan معجون أسنان toothpaste
ma'bad معبد temple (religious)
maada Taarida lil-Hasharaat مادة طاردة للحشرات insect repellent
maakeena bay' ماكينة بيع vending machine
maakeena thalj ماكينة ثلج ice machine
ma'akhadh kahrabaa' مأخذ كهرباء electric outlet
maal مال money
maaliH مالح salty
ma'loomaat معلومات information
maasiHa ماسحة scanner
maayoh مايوه swimsuit
mabna مبنى building
maDaarib golf مضارب غولف golf club
madeena مدينة town
madeena qadeema مدينة قديمة old town
madeenat al-malaahee مدينة الملاهي amusement park
madkhal مدخل access, entrance
madrassa مدرسة school
mafqood مفقود missing

maftooH مفتوح open adj
maghribee مغربي Moroccan; al-maghrib المغرب Morocco
maghsala مغسلة laundry facility
maHaarim liT-Tifl محارم للطفل baby wipe
maHabba محبة love n
maHal al'aab al-aTfaal محل ألعاب الأطفال toy store
maHal al-adawaat ar-reeyaaDeeya محل الأدوات الرياضية sporting goods store
maHal al-aHdheeya محل الأحذية shoe store
maHal al-anteekaat محل الأنتيكات antiques store
maHal al-aT'imat as-siHHeeya محل الأطعمة الصحية health food store
maHal al-hadaayaa at-tidhkaareeya محل الهدايا التذكارية gift shop, souvenir store
maHal al-kaameeraat محل الكاميرات camera store
maHal al-khuDaar محل الخضار grocery store
maHal al-malaabis محل الملابس clothing store
maHal al-mashroobaat al-kuHooleeya محل المشروبات الكحولية liquor store [off-licence BE]
maHal al-mooseeqa محل سيدات music store
maHal al-mujawharaat محل المجوهرات jeweler
maHal az-zuhoor محل الزهور florist
maHal al-Halaweeyaat محل الحلويات pastry shop
maHal al-naZaaraat محل نظارات optician
maHal tanZeef albisa محل تنظيف ألبسة dry cleaner
maHal tanZeef albisa bi-khidma dhaateeya محل تنظيف ألبسة بخدمة ذاتية laundromat [launderette BE]
maHal tijaaree محل تجاري department store
maHalee محلي domestic
maHalee محلي local
maHaTTa محطة station (railroad)
maHaTTat al-baaS محطة الباص bus station
maHaTTat al-binzeen محطة البنزين gas [petrol BE] station
maHaTTat al-qiTaar محطة القطار train station
maHaTTat metro al-anfaaq محطة مترو الأنفاق subway [underground BE] station
mahbil مهبل vagina
maHlool lil-'adasaat al-laaSiqa محلول للعدسات اللاصقة contact lens solution
maHmeeya Tabee'eeya محمية طبيعية nature preserve
majaanee مجاني free
majalla مجلة magazine
majmoo'a مجموعة group

makaan muHaaT bish-shubaak li-la'ab مكان محاط بالشباك للعب playpen

makaan mujahhaz li-istiqbaal al-mu'aaqeen مكان مجهز لاستقبال المعاقين handicapped- [disabled-BE] accessible

makhbaz مخبز bakery

makhraj مخرج exit

makhraj al-Hareeq مخرج الحريق fire door

makhraj aT-Tawaari مخرج الطوارئ emergency exit

maksoor مكسور broken

maktab مكتب office

maktab al-isti'laamaat as-seeyaaHeeya مكتب الاستعلامات السياحية tourist information office

maktab at-tadhaakir مكتب التذاكر ticket office

maktab seeyaaHa wa safar مكتب سياحة و سفر travel agency

maktab tabdeel al-'umlaat مكتب تبديل العملات currency exchange office

maktaba مكتبة bookstore, library

malaabis ملابس clothes

malaabis dakhileeya ملابس داخلية underwear

malaabis lil-ghaseel ملابس للغسيل laundry (clothes)

malaa'ib at-tinnis ملاعب تنس tennis court

mal'ab ملعب playground, stadium

mamar ممر path, trail

(bayD) mamzooj بيض ممزوج scrambled

man من who

manaadeel warqeeya مناديل ورقية tissue, paper towel

manadeel siHHeeya مناديل صحية sanitary [pad BE] napkin

mandeel lil-maa'ida منديل للمائدة napkin

maneekoor مانيكور manicure

manTaqa منطقة region

manTaqat an-nuz-haat منطقة النزهات picnic area

manTaqat at-tasawooq منطقة التسوق shopping area

maq'ad مقعد seat

maq'ad 'ala al-mamsha مقعد على الممشى aisle seat

maq'ad 'ala an-naafidha مقعد على النافذة window seat

maq'ad sayaara مقعد سيارة car seat

maqha مقهى cafe, coffee shop

maqha internet مقهى إنترنت internet cafe

marra مرة once

mareeD مريض sick [ill BE]

mareeD bir-raboo مريض بالربو asthmatic

mareeD bis-sukaree مريض بالسكري diabetic

marHaban مرحبا hi

marham مرهم cream (ointment)

markaz al-a'maal مركز الأعمال business center

markaz al-madeena مركز المدينة downtown area

markaz ash-shurTa مركز الشرطة police station

markaz at-tijaaree مركز تجاري shopping mall [centre BE]

marTabaan مرطبان jar

marwaHa مروحة fan (appliance)

masaa' مساء evening, night

masaa' al-khayr مساء الخير good afternoon, good evening

masaaj مساج massage

masbaH مسبح pool

masbaH lil-aTfaal مسبح للأطفال kiddie [paddling BE] pool

masbaH masqoof مسبح مسقوف indoor pool

mashghool مشغول busy

mashroob مشروب drink n

(qaa'imat al-) mashroobaat قائمة المشروبات drinks menu

masmooH مسموح allowed

masraH مسرح theater

masraHeeya مسرحية play n (in theater)

masrooq مسروق stolen

mata متى when

maTaar مطار airport

maT'am مطعم restaurant

maTar مطر rain n

maTbakh مطبخ kitchen

mathaana مثانة bladder

mat-Haf متحف museum

mawaad tanZeef مواد تنظيف cleaning supplies

mawaa'eed az-ziyaara مواعيد الزيارة visiting hours

maw'id موعد appointment

mawqif موقف parking, stop (on bus route)

mawqif al-baaS موقف الباص bus stop

mawqif as-sayaaraat موقف السيارات parking lot [car park BE]

mazaar مزار shrine

maZalla مظلة umbrella

mazra'a مزرعة farm

meekaaneekee ميكانيكي mechanic

meekroowayif مايكروويف microwave

metro al-anfaaq مترو الأنفاق subway [underground BE]

mi'da معدة stomach

mi'Sam معصم wrist
mi'Taf معطف coat
mi'Taf lil-maTar معطف للمطر raincoat
mibrad lil-aZaafir مبرد للأظافر nail file
miDmaar as-sibaaq مضمار السباق racetrack
miDrab مضرب racket (sports)
mifSal مفصل joint (of body)
miftaaH مفتاح key
miftaaH al-ghurfa مفتاح الغرفة room key
miHfaZa محفظة wallet
mikhadda مخدة pillow
miknasa مكنسة broom
miknasa kahrabaa'eeya مكنسة كهربائية vacuum cleaner
mikwa مكواة iron (for clothes)
mil'aqa ملعقة spoon
mil'aqa lil-'ayaar ملعقة للعيار measuring spoon
mimsaHa ممسحة mop
min من from
min faDlak من فضلك please
minfaakh منفاخ air pump
meenee baar ميني بار mini-bar
minshafa منشفة towel
miqaSS مقص scissors
miqlaah مقلاة frying pan
mirfaq مرفق elbow
miS'ad مصعد elevator [lift BE]
miSfaah مصفاة colander
mishT مشط comb
miTraqa مطرقة hammer
miyaah ghaazeeya مياه غازية sparkling water
miyaah ma'daneeya مياه معدنية still water
mookaasaan موكاسان loafer
moos موس mousse (hair)
moos al-Hilaaqa موس الحلاقة razor
mooseeqa موسيقا music
mooseeqa al-jaaz موسيقى الجاز jazz
mooseeqa al-pop موسيقى البوب pop music
mooseeqa ar-rap موسيقى الراب rap music
mooseeqa ash-sha'abeeya موسيقى شعبية folk music
mooseeqa Haya موسيقى حية live music
mooseeqa klaaseekeeya موسيقى كلاسيكية classical music
mu'aaq معاق handicapped [disabled BE]
mu'adeeya معدية ferry
mu'aqat مؤقت temporary

mu'tamar مؤتمر conference
mubakkir مبكر early
mubtadi' مبتدىء beginner
muDaadaat al-Hayawaya مضادات حيوية antibiotics
mudakhan مدخن smoked
mudda مدة period (of time)
mudeer مدير manager
mudh-hil مذهل stunning
mud-hish مدهش amazing
mu'din معد contagious
mughaadara مغادرة departure
mughaadarat al-funduq مغادرة الفندق check-out (from hotel)
mughlaq مغلق closed
muHaamee محامي lawyer
muHaasaba محاسبة invoice n
muHaasib محاسب cashier
muHawwil محوّل adapter
muhd aTfaal مهد أطفال crib [cot BE]
muHlee Sinaa'ee مُحلي صناعي artificial sweetener
mu'iddaat معدات equipment
mu'iddaat lil-ghawS معدات الغوص diving equipment
mujaffif sha'r مجفف شعر hair dryer
mujmal مُجمل total
mujawharaat مجوهرات jewelry
mukaalamat eeqaaZ مكالمة إيقاظ wake-up call
mukayyif al-hawaa' مكيف الهواء air conditioner
mukhaalafa مخالفة fine (for breaking law)
mukhayyam مخيم campsite
mulaakama ملاكمة boxing
multahib ملتهب infected
multaqee aT-Turuq ملتقى الطرق intersection
multawee ملتوي sprained
mumarriD ممرض nurse
mumill ممل boring
mumtaaz ممتاز super (fuel)
mumTir ممطر rainy
munaasib مناسب suitable
munaasib lil-meekroowayif مناسب للمايكرويف microwaveable
munaZZif منظف detergent
munfaSil منفصل separate
munHadir منحدر cliff
munHadir khaaS li-kursee al-muq'adeen منحدر خاص لكرسي المقعدين wheelchair ramp
munkhafiD منخفض low

**munhak** منهك exhausted
**munqidh** منقذ lifeguard
**muntaSif al-layl** منتصف الليل midnight
**muntaSif an-nahaar** منتصف النهار noon
**muqaabil** مقابل opposite
**muraaqaba jawaazaat as-safar** مراقبة جوازات السفر passport control
**murabeeyat aTfaal** مربية أطفال babysitter
**murtaaH** مرتاح well-rested
**musaa'ada** مساعدة help *n*
**muSaab bidaa' aS-Sura'** مصاب بداء الصرع epileptic
**muSaab bi-imsaak** مصاب بإمساك constipated
**muSaab bi-fuqr ad-damm** مصاب بفقر الدم anemic
**muSaab bi-madd an-naZar** مصاب بمد النظر far-[long- BE] sighted
**muSaab bi-qasr an-naZar** مصاب بقصر النظر near-[short- BE] sighted
**musaafir** مسافر passenger
**musabaq ad-dafa'** مسبق الدفع prepaid
**mushkila** مشكلة problem
**mushmis** مشمس sunny
**musinn** مسن senior citizen
**muslim** مسلم Muslim
**muSr** مصر Egypt
**muSree** مصري Egyptian
**musta'jil** مستعجل urgent
**mustaqeem** مستقيم straight
**mustashaar** مستشار consultant
**mustashfa** مستشفى hospital
**muta'akhir** متأخر late (time)
**muTallaq** مطلق divorced
**mutamarras** متمرس experienced
**mutaqaa'id** متقاعد retired
**mutarjim** مترجم interpreter
**mutawassiT** متوسط medium (size)
**mutazawwij** متزوج married
**muthabbit ash-sha'r** مثبت الشعر hairspray
**mutheer lil-ihtimaam** مثير للاهتمام interesting
**muzeel ar-raa'iHa** مزيل الرائحة deodorant

**N**

**naadee** نادي club
**naadee laylee** نادي ليلي nightclub
**naadee lir-raqS** نادي للرقص dance club
**naadee li-mooseeqa al-jaaz** نادي لموسيقى الجاز jazz club

**naafidha** نافذة window
**naafoora** نافورة fountain
**na'am** نعم yes
**nabaatee** نباتي vegetarian
**nadwa** ندوة seminar
**nafs** نفس same
**nahr** نهر river
**naw'eeya** نوعية quality
**naZaaraat** نظارات (eye)glasses
**naZaaraat shamseeya** نظارات شمسية sunglasses
**naZarhu Da'eef** نظره ضعيف visually impaired
**naZeef** نظيف clean *adj*
**nuHaas** نحاس copper
**nuSf** نصف half
**nuSf-kilo** نصف كيلو half-kilo
**nuskha** نسخة photocopy
**nuz-ha** نزهة walk *n*
**nuzul** نزل hostel

**O**

**oorkistraa** أوركسترا orchestra

**Q**

**qaa'at ijtimaa'aat** قاعة اجتماعات meeting room
**qaa'at al-al'aab** قاعة الألعاب arcade
**qaa'at al-Haflaat al-mooseeqeeya** قاعة الحفلات الموسيقية concert hall
**qaa'at al-mu'tamaraat** قاعة المؤتمرات convention hall
**qaa'imat an-nabeedh** قائمة النبيذ wine list
**qaa'imat aT-Ta'aam** قائمة الطعام menu
**qaa'imat Ta'aam lil-aTfaal** قائمة طعام للأطفال children's menu
**qaa'imat Ta'aam ma' al-as'aar** قائمة طعام مع الأسعار fixed-price menu
**qaarib** قارب boat
**qaarib an-najaah** قارب النجاة life boat
**qabl** قبل before
**qadam** قدم foot
**qadeem** قديم old
**qahwa** قهوة coffee
**qal'a** قلعة castle
**qalb** قلب heart
**qamaama** قمامة trash [rubbish BE]
**qameeS** قميص shirt
**qareeb** قريب close, near
**qaSdeer** قصدير pewter

qaSeer قصير short
qaSr قصر palace
qaSSa sha'r قصة شعر haircut
qaTar قطر Qatar
qaTaree قطري Qatari
qaTra قطرة drop (of liquid)
qeema قيمة value n
qeeyaas قياس size
qifl قفل lock n
qimma قمة peak n
qiT'a قطعة piece
qiT'a naqdeeya قطعة نقدية coin
qiTaar قطار train n
qiTaar saree' قطار سريع express train
qub'a قبعة hat
qudaas قداس mass (in church)
qunSuleeya قنصلية consulate
quSoor fee il-qalb قصور في القلب heart condition
quTn قطن cotton

R

radee' رديء bad
raDee' رضيع baby
rajul رجل man
rakheeS رخيص cheap
ramaadee رمادي gray
ramz al-balad رمز البلد country code
ramz al-manTaqa رمز المنطقة area code
raqaa'iq aluminyoom رقائق الألمنيوم aluminum
[kitchen BE] foil
raqm رقم number
raqm al-faaks رقم الفاكس fax number
raqm far'ee رقم فرعي extension
raqm as-sirree رقم السري PIN
raqm tilifoon رقم تلفون phone number
raqS رقص dancing
ra's رأس head
raSeef رصيف platform
rashH رشح cold n (illness)
rasm رسم fee
rasm ad-dukhool رسم الدخول admission (to
museum etc)
rasm al-khidma رسم الخدمة cover charge
rasm aS-Sarf رسم الصرف exchange fee
ratl رطل pound (weight)
ri'a رئة lung

riDaa'a رضاعة baby bottle
ridfayn ردفين buttock
riHla رحلة excursion, trip
riHla bil-qaarib رحلة بالقارب boat trip
riHla jaweeya رحلة جوية flight
risaala رسالة letter
risaala رسالة message
rool رول roll
roomaansee رومانسي romantic
rukba ركبة knee
rukhSa qeeyaada رخصة قيادة driver's license
rukoob ad-daraaja ركوب الدراجة cycling
ruqba رقبة neck
rusoom jumrukeeya رسوم جمركية duty (customs)

S

saa'a Haa'iTeeya ساعة حائطية clock
saa'a ساعة hour
saa'a yad ساعة يد watch n
Saaboon صابون soap
saaHat al-madeena ساحة المدينة town square
SaaHib صاحب boyfriend
SaaHiba صاحبة girlfriend
saa'iH سائح tourist
saa'il li-ghaseel aS-SuHoon سائل لغسيل الصحون
dishwashing [washing-up BE] liquid
saakhin ساخن hot
Saala seenimaa صالة سينما movie theater
Saaloon koowaafeer صالون كوافير hair salon
saawnaa ساونا sauna
saaq ساق leg
SabaaH صباح morning
SabaaH al-khayr صباح الخير good morning
Sabee صبي boy
Sabgha صبغة color
sadaadaat quTneeya lis-sayyidaat
سدادات قطنية للسيدات tampon
Sadeeq صديق friend
Sadr صدر chest
sa'eed سعيد happy
Saff صف class (in school)
Sagheer صغير little, small
saHab min al-Hisaab سحب من الحساب debit
SaHeeH صحيح right, correct
sahil سهل easy
SaHn صحن dish, plate

SaHraa' صحراء desert
sakaakir سكاكر candy [sweets BE]
saakhun akthar min al-laazim ساخن أكثر من اللازم overheated
salaalim kahrabaa'eeya سلالم كهربائية escalator
Salaat صلاة service (in church)
salb سلب mugging
Saloon tajmeel صالون تجميل nail salon
samaa'aat سماعات headphone
sami' Da'eef سمع ضعيف hearing impaired
sam سم poison
sana سنة year
Sandal صندل sandals
centimeter (santimitir) سنتمتر centimeter
sa'oodee سعودي Saudi; as-sa'oodeeya السعودية Saudi Arabia
Saraaf aalee صراف آلي ATM
saree' سريع fast
sareer سرير bed
sareer aTfaal سرير أطفال crib [cot BE]
sareer mufrad سرير مفرد single bed
sareer muzdawwaj سرير مزدوج double bed
sareer qaabil liT-Tawwi سرير قابل للطوي cot [campbed BE]
sawt a'la صوت أعلى louder
sayaara سيارة car
sayaara fakhma سيارة فخمة luxury car
sayaara musta'jara سيارة مستأجرة rental [hire BE] car
sayaarat al-is'aaf سيارة الإسعاف ambulance
Saydleeya صيدلية pharmacy [chemist BE]
see dee سي دي CD
seegaar سيجار cigar
silseeyoos سلسيوس Celsius
shaab شاب young
shaaHina qaaTira شاحنة قاطرة tow truck
sha'r شعر hair
shaari' شارع street
shaaTee' شاطئ beach
shadeed al-inHidaar شديد الانحدار steep
shafaraat al-Hilaaqa شفرات الحلاقة razor blade
shahaada شهادة certificate
shahr شهر month
shajara شجرة tree
shakwa شكوى complaint
shalaal شلال waterfall
shama' khaT al-beekeenee شمع خط البيكيني bikini wax

shaamboo شامبو shampoo
shams شمس sun
sharaashif شراشف sheet
shareeHa شريحة slice
sharq شرق east
shawka شوكة fork
sheek شيك check (payment) [cheque BE]
sheek seeyaaHee شيك سياحي travelers check [traveller's cheque BE]
shibshib شبشب slipper
shiffa شفة lip
shimaal شمال north
shiqqa شقة apartment
shirka ta'meen شركة تأمين insurance company
shoort شورت shorts
shukran شكراً thank you
shurTa الشرطة police
siHHa صحة health
sijaa'ir سجائر cigarette
sikeen سكين knife
silla سلة basket
sinn سن tooth
si'r سعر price, charge (cost)
si'r aS-Sarf سعر الصرف exchange rate
si'r muHaddad سعر محدد fixed-price
sirqa سرقة theft
sirwaal daakhilee سروال داخلي briefs [underpants BE]
sitrat an-najaah سترة النجاة life jacket
siwaar سوار bracelet
SMS اس ام اس text message
snorkel (shnurkil) شنركل snorkeling equipment
Sooda صودا soda
soodaanee سوداني Sudanese; as-soodaan السودان Sudan
Soof صوف wool
soobir maarkit سوبر ماركت supermarket
sooq سوق market
Soora صورة photograph
sooree سوري Syrian
sooriyaa سوريا Syria
spa (sbaa) سبا spa
su'aal سعال cough n
su'aal سؤال question
Sudaa' صداع headache
Sundooq صندوق package

**Sundooq al-bareed** صندوق البريد mailbox [postbox BE]
**Su'ub** صعب difficult
**Suwwar dijeetaal** صور دجيتال digital photo

# T

**Ta'aam** طعام food
**Ta'aam lir-raDa'** طعام للرضع baby food, formula
**Ta'aam mujammad** طعام مجمد frozen food
**ta'Tul** تعطل breakdown
**ta'baan** تعبان tired
**Taabi'** طابع stamp n
**Taabiq al-arDee** طابق أرضي ground floor
**taa'ih** تائه lost
**Taa'ira** طائرة airplane
**ta'jeer as-sayaaraat** تأجير السيارات car rental [hire BE]
**taalee** تالي next
**Taalib** طالب student
**taalif** تالف damaged
**ta'meen** تأمين insurance
**ta'reekh** تاريخ date (on calendar)
**ta'Tal** تعطل broke down
**Taawila** طاولة table
**Tabaq al-yawm** طبق اليوم menu of the day
**aTbaaq iDaafee** أطباق إضافية side dish
**tabdeel al-'umlaat** تبديل العملات currency exchange
**tabdeel Taa'ira** تبديل طائرة connection (in travel)
**Tabeeb** طبيب doctor
**Tabeeb asnaan** طبيب أسنان dentist
**Tabeeb aTfaal** طبيب أطفال pediatrician
**Tabeeb nisaa'ee** طبيب نسائي gynecologist
**tadfi'a** تدفئة heater [heating BE]
**tadhkara** تذكرة ticket
**tadhkarat iliktrooneeya** تذكرة الكترونية e-ticket
**tadhkara lil-baaS** تذكرة للباص bus ticket
**tadhkara dhihaab wa 'awda** تذكرة ذهاب و عودة round-trip [return BE] ticket
**TafH jildee** طفح جلدي rash n
**taHmeeD** تحميض develop (film)
**taHweela** تحويلة detour
**takhdeer** تخدير anesthesia
**takhfeeD** تخفيض discount
**takhreem** تخريم lace
**taaksee** تاكسي taxi
**Talb tawSeel** طلب توصيل hitchhike
**tanoora** تنورة skirt
**tanZeef al-wajah** تنظيف الوجه facial n

**taqleedee** تقليدي traditional
**Taqm** طقم suit (clothing)
**taqreer ash-shurTa** تقرير الشرطة police report
**Taqs** طقس weather
**Tareeq** طريق road, route
**Tareeq aakhar** طريق آخر alternate route
**Tareeq lil-khuyool** طريق للخيول horsetrack
**Tareeq bi-rasm muroor** طريق برسم مرور toll road
**Tareeq saree'** طريق سريع highway [motorway BE]
**tasawooq** تسوق shopping
**tashanuj** تشنج cramp
**tashgheel** تشغيل on
**tasjeel sayaara** تسجيل سيارة vehicle registration
**tasleeya** تسلية entertainment
**taSreeH jumrukee** تصريح جمركي customs declaration form
**taSweer bil-flaash** تصوير بالفلاش flash photography
**taTreef sha'r** تطريف شعر trim (haircut)
**Tawaal al-layl** طوال الليل overnight
**Tawaari'** طوارئ emergency
**tawqu'aat aT-Taqs** توقعات الطقس forecast
**Taweel** طويل long
**Tayr** طير bird
**tee sheert** تي شرت T-shirt
**tilifizyoon** تلفزيون TV
**tinnis** تنس tennis
**teerminaal** تيرمنال terminal (airport)
**thaddee** ثدي breast
**thalj** ثلج ice
**thallaaja** ثلاجة refrigerator
**Tifl** طفل child
**tilifoon** تلفون phone n
**till** تل hill
**toonis** تونس Tunisia
**toonisee** تونسي Tunisian
**toowaaleet** تواليت restroom [toilet BE]
**toowaaleet khaaS lil-mu'aaqeen** تواليت خاص للمعاقين disabled restroom [toilet BE]
**toowaaleet kimiyaa'ee** تواليت كيميائي chemical toilet
**tughaadir** تغادر leave (airplane)
**turaDDi'** ترضع breastfeed
**Turuq as-sayr** طرق السير walking route

# U

**'uboor mushaa** عبور مشاة pedestrian crosswalk [crossing BE]

**udhn** أذن ear
**ujrat iDaafeeya** أجرة إضافية surcharge
**ukht** أخت sister
**'ulba** علبة box
**'umaan** عمان Oman
**'umaanee** عماني Omani
**'umla** عملة currency
**umm** أم mother
**'umr** عمر age
**'unwaan** عنوان address
**'unwaan iliktroonee** عنوان الكتروني e-mail address
**'uqd** عقد necklace
**urdunee** أردني Jordanian; **al-urdun** الأردن Jordan
**usboo'** أسبوع week
**usboo'ee** أسبوعي weekly
**ustraalee** أسترالي Australian
**ustraaleeyaa** أستراليا Australia
**'uTla nihaayat al-usboo'** عطلة نهاية الأسبوع weekend
**'uTr** عطر perfume
**'uTr ba'ad al-Halaaqa** عطر بعد الحلاقة aftershave

## V

**van (faan)** فان (فان) van

## W

**waadee** وادي valley
**waaDiH** واضح clear adj
**waaHid** واحد one
**waaqee dhikree** واقي ذكري condom
**waaqee shamsee** واقي شمسي sunblock
**waasi'** واسع loose (fit)
**waHdee** وحدي on my own
**wajabaat aSghar lil-aTfaal** وجبات أصغر للأطفال children's portion
**wajah** وجه face
**wajba** وجبة meal
**wakaala** وكالة agency
**walaa'a** ولاعة lighter (cigarettes)
**waqt** وقت time
**waraq** ورق paper
**waraq toowaaleet** ورق تواليت toilet paper
**waSfa Tibeeya** وصفة طبية prescription
**wazn amti'a zaa'id** وزن أمتعة زائد excess luggage
**wisikh** وسخ dirty

## Y

**ya'kul** يأكل eat
**ya'mal** يعمل work v
**ya'nee** يعني mean v
**yaaqa mudawwara** ياقة مدورة crew neck
**yab'ath SMS** يبعث اس ام اس text v
**yabda'** يبدأ begin, start v
**yabee'** يبيع sell
**yaboos** يبوس kiss v
**yabtala'** يبتلع swallow v
**yad** يد hand
**yadfa'** يدفع pay v
**yadh-hab** يذهب go
**yadkhil** يدخل insert v
**yadkhul** يدخل enter
**yadkhul 'ala al-internet** يدخل على الإنترنت log on
**yadkhul fee is-sayr** يدخل في السير merge
**yadrus** يدرس study v
**ya'eesh** يعيش live v
**yafham** يفهم understand
**yafHaS** يفحص check v
**yafqud** يفقد lose (something)
**yaftaH** يفتح open v
**yaghliq** يغلق close v
**yaghTus** يغطس dive v
**yaHjuz** يحجز reserve v
**yaHSal** يحصل happen
**yajid** يجد reach (person)
**yajlib** يجلب bring
**yajlis** يجلس sit
**yakhla'** يخلع extract v (tooth)
**yakhruj** يخرج exit v
**yakoon** يكون be
**yal'ab** يلعب play v
**yaltaqee** يلتقي meet v
**yamanee** يمني Yemeni; **al-yaman** اليمن Yemen
**yameen** يمين right (direction)
**yamHi** يمحي delete v
**yanSaH** ينصح recommend
**yantahee** ينتهي end v
**yantaZar** ينتظر wait v
**yanzif** ينزف bleed
**yanzil** ينزل get off (a train/bus/subway)
**yanzil** ينزل descend, stay v
**ya'ood** يعود return v
**yaqbal** يقبل accept

**yaqees** يقيس fit v (clothing)
**yaqful** يقفل lock up
**yaqif** يقف stop
**yaqood** يقود drive v
**yaqTa' al-ittiSaal** يقطع الاتصال disconnect
**yaquSS** يقص cut v (hair)
**yarquS** يرقص dance v
**yasaar** يسار left (direction)
**yaSaff** يصف park v (car)
**yasbaH** يسبح swim v
**yas-Hab** يسحب withdraw, pull
**yash'al** يشعل light v (cigarette)
**yash'al** يشعل turn on (light)
**yash-Han** يشحن recharge v
**yashoof** يشوف look v
**yashoof** يشوف see
**yashrab** يشرب drink v
**yashtaree** يشتري buy v
**yash'ur bi-duwaar** يشعر بدوار dizzy
**yash'ur bi-ghathayaan** يشعر بغثيان nauseous
**yaSil** يصل arrive
**yasriq** يسرق steal
**yasta'jir** يستأجر rent v (hire BE)
**yastakhdim** يستخدم use v
**yastamata'** يستمتع enjoy
**yastaqbil** يستقبل receive v
**yata'khar** يتأخر delay n
**yatadhawwaq** يتذوق taste v
**yatakallam** يتكلم speak
**yatanaffas** يتنفس breath
**yataqaya** يتقيأ vomiting
**yatasaaqaT ath-thalj** يتساقط الثلج snowy
**yaTba'** يطبع print v
**yaTbukh** يطبخ cook v
**yaTfa'** يطفئ turn off (light)
**yaTlub** يطلب charge v, order
**yatruk** يترك leave v (deposit)
**yattaSil** يتصل call (telephone)
**yattaSil** يتصل contact v, connect, phone
**yattaSil laaHiqan** يتصل لاحقاً call back
**yazoor** يزور visit v
**yiDghuT** يضغط dial v
**yimlaa** يملأ fill out (form)
**yimlaa** يملأ fill up (tank)
**yawm** يوم day
**yawqiZ** يوقظ wake (person)

**yu'Tee** يعطي give
**yu'aanee min al-Hasaaseeya** يعاني من الحساسية allergic
**yu'aaniq** يعانق hug v
**yu'akid** يؤكد confirm
**yu'lim** يؤلم hurt v
**yu'aSar fee il-ghasaala** يعصر في الغسالة tumble dry
**yubaddil** يبدل change (money); exchange v; transfer
**yuballigh 'an** يبلغ عن report v
**yughaadir** يغادر leave (go away)
**yughassal** يغسل wash v
**yughayir** يغير change v
**yuHibb** يحب like, love v (someone)
**yukallif** يكلف cost v
**yukassir** يكسر break (tooth, bone)
**yukhayyam** يخيم camp v
**yukhbir** يخبر notify
**yuktub** يكتب write (down)
**yunqush** ينقش engrave
**yuqaddim** يقدم introduce **yuraafiq** يرافق accompany
**yuraqi'** يرقع patch
**yuree** يري show v
**yursil** يرسل send
**yusakhin** يسخن warm v
**yuSalliH** يصلح repair v
**yutarjim** يترجم translate
**yuT'im** يطعم feed v (baby)
**yuwaqi'** يوقع sign v

## Z

**zaa'idat ad-doodeeya** زائدة دودية appendix
**zaaweeya** زاوية corner
**zahra** زهرة flower
**zahree** زهري pink
**zameel** زميل colleague
**Zarf** ظرف envelope
**zayt** زيت oil
**zibda** زبدة butter
**zawj** زوج husband
**zawja** زوجة wife
**zawraq** زورق motorboat
**zubdeeya** زبدية bowl
**Zuhr** ظهر back (of body)
**zujaaj** زجاج glass (material)
**zujaaja** زجاجة bottle

# INDEX

**Berlitz** pocket guide

# OMAN

**Third Edition 2018**

**Editor:** Sian Marsh
**Author:** Chris Bradley
**Head of Production:** Rebeka Davies
**Picture Editor:** Tom Smyth
**Cartography Update:** Carte
**Update Production:** Apa Digital
**Photography Credits:** Chris Bradley/Apa
Publications 4TC, 4TL, 5T, 5TC, 5MC, 5MC,
5M, 6L, 6R, 7, 11, 12, 16, 30, 34, 37, 39, 40,
42, 48, 50, 51, 52, 54, 56, 58, 62, 64, 66, 67,
68, 72, 75, 77, 78, 80, 82, 84, 87, 93, 94, 95,
99; Clay Perry/Apa Publications 38; Corbis
18, 21, 23; Elvis John Ferrao 4MC; Getty
Images 1, 15, 47, 61; Hyatt 90; iStock 7R,
102; Kevin Cummins/Apa Publications 24,
26, 28, 32, 69, 70, 74, 89, 97, 100, 104; Oman
Tourism 4ML, 45; Shutterstock 5M
**Cover Picture:** iStock

**Distribution**
**UK, Ireland and Europe:** Apa Publications
(UK) Ltd; sales@insightguides.com
**United States and Canada:** Ingram
Publisher Services; ips@ingramcontent.com
**Australia and New Zealand:** Woodslane;
info@woodslane.com.au
**Southeast Asia:** Apa Publications (SN) Pte;
singaporeoffice@insightguides.com
**Worldwide:** Apa Publications (UK) Ltd;
sales@insightguides.com

**Special Sales, Content Licensing
and CoPublishing**
Insight Guides can be purchased in bulk
quantities at discounted prices. We can
create special editions, personalised jackets
and corporate imprints tailored to your
needs. sales@insightguides.com;
www.insightguides.biz

**Contact us**
Every effort has been made to provide
accurate information in this publication,
but changes are inevitable. The publisher
cannot be responsible for any resulting loss,
inconvenience or injury. We would appreciate
it if readers would call our attention to any
errors or outdated information. We also
welcome your suggestions; please contact
us at: berlitz@apaguide.co.uk
www.insightguides.com/berlitz

# Berlitz®

speaking your language

**phrase book & dictionary**
**phrase book & CD**

**Available in:** Arabic, Brazilian Portuguese*, Burmese*, Cantonese
Chinese, Croatian, Czech*, Danish*, Dutch, English, Filipino, Finnish*, French,
German, Greek, Hebrew*, Hindi*, Hungarian*, Indonesian, Italian, Japanese,
Korean, Latin American Spanish, Malay, Mandarin Chinese, Mexican Spanish,
Norwegian, Polish, Portuguese, Romanian*, Russian, Spanish, Swedish, Thai,
Turkish, Vietnamese
*Book only